I0415704

January 2012

NATIONAL CREDIT UNION ADMINISTRATION

Earlier Actions Are Needed to Better Address Troubled Credit Unions

GAO
Accountability * Integrity * Reliability

GAO-12-247

GAO
Accountability * Integrity * Reliability

Highlights

Highlights of GAO-12-247, a report to congressional committees

NATIONAL CREDIT UNION ADMINISTRATION

Earlier Actions Are Needed to Better Address Troubled Credit Unions

Why GAO Did This Study

Corporate credit unions (corporates)—financial institutions that provide liquidity and other services to the more than 7,400 federally insured credit unions—experienced billions in financial losses since the financial crisis began in 2007, contributing to failures throughout the credit union system and losses to the National Credit Union Share Insurance Fund (NCUSIF). Since 1998, Congress has required the National Credit Union Administration (NCUA), the federal regulator of the credit union system, to take prompt corrective action (PCA) to identify and address the financial deterioration of federally insured natural person credit unions (credit unions) and minimize potential losses to the NCUSIF. Legislation enacted in 2011 requires GAO to examine NCUA's supervision of the credit union system and use of PCA. This report examines (1) the failures of corporates and credit unions since 2008, (2) NCUA's response to the failures, and (3) the effectiveness of NCUA's use of PCA. To do this work, GAO analyzed agency and industry financial data and material loss reviews, reviewed regulations, and interviewed agency officials and trade organizations.

What GAO Recommends

NCUA should (1) provide its Office Inspector General the necessary documentation to verify loss estimates and (2) consider additional triggers for PCA that would require early and forceful regulatory action and make recommendations to Congress on how to modify PCA, as appropriate. NCUA agreed with both recommendations.

View GAO-12-247. For more information, contact A. Nicole Clowers at (202) 512-8678 or clowersa@gao.gov.

What GAO Found

From January 1, 2008, through June 30, 2011, 5 corporates and 85 credit unions failed. As of January 1, 2008, the 5 failed corporates were some of the largest—accounting for 75 percent of all corporate assets—but the 85 failed credit unions were relatively small—accounting for less than 1 percent of total credit union assets. GAO found poor investment and business strategies contributed to the corporate failures. Specifically, the failed corporates overconcentrated their investments in private-label, mortgage-backed securities (MBS) and invested substantially more in private-label MBS than corporates that did not fail. GAO also found that poor management was the primary reason the 85 credit unions failed. In addition, NCUA's Office of Inspector General has reported that NCUA's examination and enforcement processes did not result in strong and timely actions to avert the failure of these institutions.

NCUA took multiple actions to stabilize, resolve, and reform the corporate system. NCUA used existing funding sources, such as the NCUSIF, and new funding sources, including the Temporary Corporate Credit Union Stabilization Fund (Stabilization Fund), to stabilize and provide liquidity to the corporates. NCUA placed the failing corporates into conservatorship and liquidated certain poor performing assets. In order to decrease losses from the corporates' failures, NCUA established a securitization program to provide long-term funding for assets formerly held in the portfolios of failed corporates by issuing NCUA-guaranteed notes. To address weaknesses highlighted by the crisis, in 2010, NCUA issued regulations to prohibit investment in private-label MBS, established a PCA framework for corporates, and introduced new governance provisions. NCUA considered credit unions' ability to repay borrowings from Treasury and included measures to reduce moral hazard, minimize the cost of resolving the corporates, and protect taxpayers. While NCUA has estimated the losses to the Stabilization Fund, it could not provide adequate documentation to allow NCUA's Office of Inspector General or GAO to verify their completeness and reasonableness. Without well-documented cost information, NCUA faces questions about its ability to effectively estimate the total costs of the failures and determine whether the credit unions will be able to pay for these losses.

GAO's analysis of PCA and other NCUA enforcement actions highlights opportunities for improvement. For credit unions subject to PCA, GAO found those credit unions that did not fail were more likely subject to earlier PCA action—that is, before their capital levels deteriorated to the significantly or critically undercapitalized levels—than failed credit unions. GAO also found that for many of the failed credit unions, other enforcement actions were initiated either too late or not at all. GAO has previously noted that the effectiveness of PCA for banks is limited because of its reliance on capital, which can lag behind other indicators of financial health. GAO examined other potential financial indicators for credit unions, including measures of asset quality and liquidity, and found a number of indicators that could provide early warning of credit union distress. Incorporating such indicators into the PCA framework could improve its effectiveness.

_____ **United States Government Accountability Office**

Contents

Figures

Abbreviations

BAM	Board Action Memorandum
CAMEL	Capital Adequacy, Asset Quality, Management, Earnings and Liquidity
CLF	Central Liquidity Facility
CU-HARP	Credit Union Homeowners Affordability Relief Program
CU-SIP	Credit Union System Investment Program
CUSO	Credit Union Service Organization
DOR	document of resolution
MBS	mortgage-backed securities
MBL	member business loan
MLR	material loss review
NCUA	National Credit Union Administration
NCUSIF	National Credit Union Share Insurance Fund
NSPM	National Supervision Policy Manual
OIG	Office of Inspector General
PCA	prompt corrective action

January 4, 2012

The Honorable Tim Johnson
Chairman
The Honorable Richard C. Shelby
Ranking Minority
Committee on Banking, Housing,
   and Urban Affairs
United States Senate

The Honorable Spencer Bachus
Chairman
The Honorable Barney Frank
Ranking Member
Committee on Financial Services
House of Representatives

The credit union system has undergone a period of financial turmoil since the financial crisis that began in 2007, resulting in an estimated $5 billion to $10 billion in losses to the 7,400 credit unions and the institutions that support them, known as corporate credit unions (corporates).[1] Corporates are financial institutions whose members are credit unions, not individuals, and that provide credit unions with payment services, investment opportunities, and other forms of credit, should credit unions face liquidity needs. The corporates experienced significant financial losses during the financial crisis that in turn contributed to losses to the National Credit Union Share Insurance Fund (NCUSIF). NCUSIF covers the balance of each member's account, up to the insurance limit, including principal and posted dividends through the date of any failure.[2] The National Credit Union Administration (NCUA) is responsible for

---

[1] Estimates were based on National Credit Union Administration estimated losses to the Temporary Corporate Credit Union Stabilization Fund (Stabilization Fund) (June 30, 2011) and the National Credit Union Share Insurance Fund (Sept. 30, 2011). NCUA had not issued its full financial audit statement for 2010, as of December 19, 2011, to include losses from its Stabilization Fund. The NCUA 2010 Financial Statement Audit for Temporary Corporate Credit Union Stabilization Fund was released on December 27, 2011. There were 7,400 credit unions as of June 2010.

[2] NCUSIF provides primary deposit insurance for member shares up to $250,000.

administering NCUSIF, as well as for overseeing federally insured credit unions, which includes corporates.

To minimize losses to NCUSIF, NCUA is required to take prompt corrective action (PCA) to identify and address declining capital in credit unions. Specifically, NCUA is required to classify credit unions into one of five capital categories, and take mandatory and increasingly severe supervisory actions, such as restrictions on asset growth, as a credit union's capital deteriorates. Prior to the 2007-2009 financial crisis, PCA for credit unions was largely untested. In particular, after the passage of the Credit Union Membership Access Act, which established PCA for credit unions, the growth in the economy meant that the financial condition of credit unions was generally strong.[3] However, as the financial crisis unfolded, the financial condition of many credit unions declined, testing the effectiveness of PCA on a widespread basis.

Legislation enacted in January 2011 requires us to examine NCUA's supervision of the credit union system and use of PCA.[4] This report examines (1) what is known about the causes of any failures among corporates and credit unions since 2008; (2) the steps that NCUA has taken to resolve these failures and the extent to which its actions were designed to protect taxpayers, avoid moral hazard, and minimize the cost of corporate resolutions;[5] and (3) the effectiveness of NCUA's use of PCA and other enforcement actions. This report also contains information on NCUA's implementation of its Office of Inspector General (OIG) recommendations in appendix I.

To determine what is known about the causes of failures among corporates and credit unions, we obtained and analyzed NCUA documents, including the OIG's Material Loss Reviews (MLR), NCUA postmortem reports, regional examiner reports, and Board Action

---

[3]Pub. L. No. 105-219, 112. Stat. 913 (1998).

[4]An act to clarify National Credit Union Administration authority to make Temporary Corporate Credit Union Stabilization Fund expenditures without borrowing from the Treasury, Pub. L. No. 111-382, § 4(a), 124 Stat. 4134, 4135 (2011).

[5]Moral hazard occurs when a party insulated from risk may behave differently than it would behave if it were fully exposed to the risk. In the context of NCUA's actions to stabilize the credit union system, moral hazard may occur when market participants expect similar emergency actions in future crises, thereby weakening their incentives to manage risks properly.

Memorandums (BAM).[6] As of November 30, 2011, OIG had issued MLRs on 5 corporates and 11 credit unions, and NCUA had conducted 15 postmortem reviews on credit unions that failed since 2008. We obtained and analyzed NCUA data related to conservatorships and resolution actions from January 2008 to June 30, 2011, to determine the number and causes of corporate and credit union failures. To corroborate this information, we assessed the asset size and investment concentrations for all failed and nonfailed corporates using data from SNL Financial—a financial institution database. We assessed the reliability of certain data from this database, which is obtained from credit union financial reports submitted to the credit union regulators (referred to as call reports), and found the data to be sufficiently reliable for calculating ratios for our analysis.[7] We further calculated ratios of credit union member business lending as a percentage of total loans for the failed credit unions and their peers that did not fail. We interviewed officials in NCUA's OIG, Office of Corporate Credit Unions, Office of Capital Markets, and Office of Examination and Insurance to gain their perspectives on the causes of the corporate and credit union failures.

To assess the steps that NCUA has taken to stabilize, resolve, and reform the credit union system, we analyzed information from BAMs; MLRs; NCUA's Corporate System Stabilization and Resolution Plan; NCUA's 2008, 2009, and 2010 annual reports; audited financial statements and other cost estimate information; and NCUA-commissioned reports; in addition to testimonies at relevant congressional hearings and planning documents.[8] We also analyzed NCUA's proposed and final rules to determine actions taken to reform the

---

[6]The Federal Credit Union Act, as amended, requires the OIG to conduct an MLR of an insured credit union if the loss to NCUSIF exceeds $25 million and an amount equal to 10 percent of the total assets of the credit union at the time at which the NCUA Board initiated assistance or was appointed liquidating agent. NCUA, as a matter of policy, separately prepares postmortems for failed credit unions where the net loss to NCUSIF is between $2 million and $25 million.

[7]A quarterly listing of summarized accounts is collected from all federally insured credit unions, referred to as the 5300 Call Report. The corporates submit financial information, including Statement of Financial Condition, Income Statement, Liquidity Report, Delinquent Loans, Investments, and other financial data on the Corporate 5310 Report, referred to as a call report.

[8]NCUA commissioned a number of reports to assist them in estimating losses and determining options for addressing the failures of the corporates, including reports by Kamakura Corporation, PIMCO, and Barclay's Capital.

system. We interviewed officials in NCUA's OIG, Office of Corporate Credit Unions, Office of Capital Markets, Office of Examination and Insurance, and Office of General Counsel to discuss NCUA's response to corporate and credit union failures, and efforts to stabilize, resolve, and reform the system.

To determine the regulatory actions NCUA has taken to address deteriorating credit unions, we reviewed NCUA's regulatory information that included Capital Adequacy, Asset Quality, Management, Earnings and Liquidity (CAMEL) ratings, enforcement action data, and PCA-related actions over a 2-year period prior to each credit union failure.[9] To assess the outcomes of PCA, we analyzed the instances and dates of CAMEL downgrades, enforcement actions taken, and PCA-related actions to determine whether and when NCUA examiners took actions for distressed credit unions subject to PCA from January 1, 2006, through June 30, 2011. We assessed the data reliability of NCUA's enforcement data and found these data to be sufficiently reliable for this analysis. We reviewed a variety of indicators of credit unions' financial condition, such as return on assets, operating expenses, and liquid assets as an early warning of financial distress. We selected these leading indicators based on the OIG's MLRs, NCUA's postmortem studies, and our previous work on bank regulation related to PCA.[10] Using these indicators and data from SNL Financial, we compared the performance of failed credit unions to peer credit unions that did not fail. We found the data to be sufficiently reliable for our purposes. We also verified the status of NCUA's implementation of OIG recommendations through a documentation review and interviews with NCUA OIG officials and relevant NCUA officials. Appendix II contains additional details of our scope and methodology.

We conducted this performance audit from May 2011 to December 2011 in accordance with generally accepted government auditing standards. Those standards require that we plan and perform the audit to obtain sufficient, appropriate evidence to provide a reasonable basis for our

---

[9]NCUA rates credit unions using the CAMEL rating system, which stands for capital adequacy, asset quality, management, earnings and liquidity. The ratings are on a scale of 1 to 5, with 1 being the best and 5 the worst.

[10]GAO, *Bank Regulation: Modified Prompt Corrective Action Framework Would Improve Effectiveness*, GAO-11-612 (Washington D.C.: June 23, 2011).

findings and conclusions based on our audit objectives. We believe that the evidence obtained provides a reasonable basis for our findings and conclusions based on our audit objectives.

Background

Credit unions are tax-exempt, cooperative financial institutions run by member-elected, primarily volunteer boards. To build capital, credit unions do not issue stock; they are not-for-profit entities that build capital by retained earnings. Their tax-exempt status and cooperative, not-for-profit structure separate credit unions from other depository institutions. Like banks and thrifts, credit unions are either federally or state chartered.

Credit Union System

Prior to the financial crisis, the credit union system consisted of three tiers, as shown in figure 1. As of December 31, 2007, there were 8,101 credit unions, 27 corporate credit unions, and 1 wholesale corporate credit union—U.S. Central Federal Credit Union (U.S. Central). Credit unions are owned by individual members (natural persons) who make share deposits and are provided with products and services, such as lending, investments, and payment processing. Credit unions are subject to limits on their membership because members must have a "common bond"—for example, working for the same employer or living in the same community.[11] Corporates are owned by and serve credit unions. Corporates provide payment processing services and loans for liquidity purposes and serve as repositories for credit unions' excess liquidity, among other things.[12] In particular, when loan demand is low or deposits are high, credit unions generally invest excess liquidity in corporates and then withdraw funds when loan demand is high or deposits are low. Corporates meet liquidity needs with member deposits and by borrowing

---

[11]As we reported in 2003, over the years the common bond requirements have become less restrictive and credit unions can now form multiple-bond credit unions. Members can also retain their credit union membership even after the basis for the original bond has ended. For more information, see GAO, *Credit Unions: Financial Condition Has Improved, but Opportunities Exist to Enhance Oversight and Share Insurance Management*, GAO-04-91 (Washington, D.C.: Oct. 27, 2003).

[12]Payment processing services include debit and credit card settlements, automated clearinghouse items, check processing, and wire transfers.

from U.S. Central, capital markets, or the Federal Home Loan Banks.[13] Corporates primarily owned by U.S. Central, which functioned as a corporate for the corporates, provide the same depository and other services that corporates provide to credit unions. U.S. Central was the agent group representative for the Central Liquidity Facility (CLF), which we discuss later in this section. U.S. Central also acted as an aggregator of corporate credit union funds, which allowed them better access to the markets at better rates.

Figure 1: Credit Union System, as of December 31, 2007

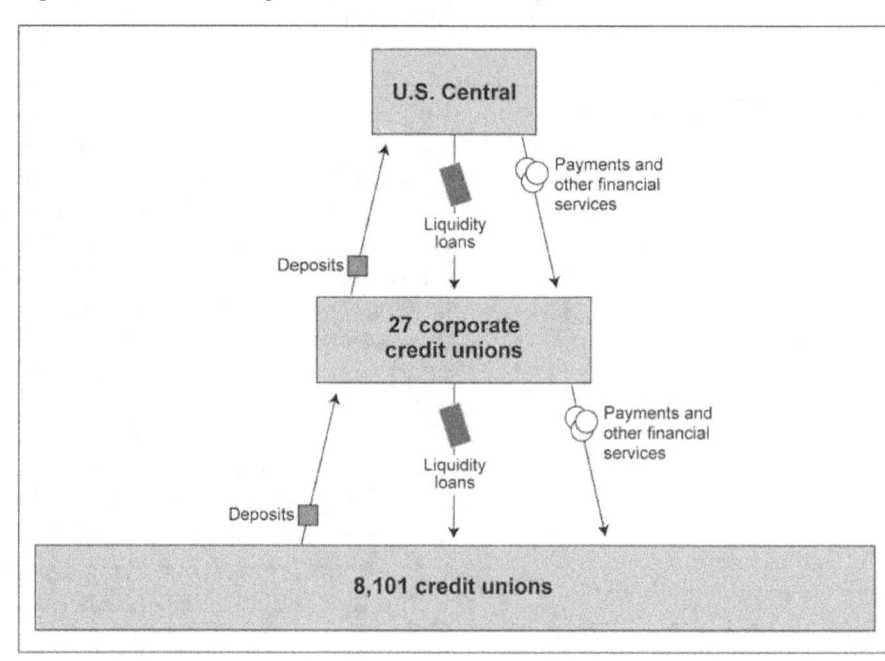

Source: GAO analysis of NCUA data.

While the corporate system—including both U.S. Central and the corporates—was designed to meet the needs of credit unions, the corporates face competition from other corporates and financial institutions that can provide needed services. For instance, credit unions

---

[13]Federal Home Loan Banks are regional cooperatives owned by members that include community banks, credit unions, community development financial institutions, and insurance companies. Federal Home Loan Banks make loans to members known as "advances."

may also obtain loans and payment processing from Federal Reserve Banks.[14] In addition, credit unions can obtain investment products and services from broker-dealers or investment firms rather than corporates. Credit union service organizations (CUSO) also compete with corporates and offer, among other things, investments and payment processing.[15] As we reported in 2004, corporates seek to provide their members with higher returns on their deposits and lower costs on products and services than can be obtained individually elsewhere.[16]

Credit unions and corporates are insured by NCUSIF, which provides primary deposit insurance for 98 percent of the nation's credit unions and corporates.[17] NCUA administers NCUSIF, collects premiums from credit unions and corporates to fund NCUSIF, and ensures that all credit unions operate in a safe and sound manner. NCUA is required to maintain NCUSIF's equity ratio at a percentage of no less than 1.2 percent and not more than 1.5 percent of insured shares.[18] In addition, NCUA provides oversight of the CLF, which lends to credit unions experiencing unusual loss of liquidity.[19] Credit unions can borrow directly from the CLF or

---

[14]The Federal Reserve System's discount window extends credit to generally sound depository institutions, including credit unions, as a short-term source of funds.

[15]CUSOs and third-party vendors differ in that CUSOs primarily serve and are owned by credit unions or corporates but maintain a separate legal identity from the credit union or corporate. NCUA specifies the types of activities a CUSO may undertake but does not regulate CUSOs directly. Most credit unions are limited in how much they can loan to or invest in CUSOs, generally up to 1 percent of assets.

[16]For more information see: GAO, *Corporate Credit Unions: Competitive Environment May Stress Financial Condition, Posing Challenges for NCUA Oversight*, GAO-04-977 (Washington, D.C.: Sept. 10, 2004).

[17]According to information provided by American Share Insurance, the sole private credit union insurer, as of September 30, 2011, there were 145 privately insured credit unions in nine states, representing about 2 percent of all credit unions in the country. The Emergency Economic Stabilization Act of 2008 temporarily increased the members' share insurance amount with NCUSIF from $100,000 to $250,000 from October 3, 2008, through December 31, 2009. The Helping Families Save Their Homes Act of 2009 extended the temporary increase through December 31, 2013, and the Dodd-Frank Wall Street Reform and Consumer Protection Act made the increase permanent.

[18]12 U.S.C. §1782(h)(4).

[19]Created by Congress in 1978, CLF membership is voluntary for credit unions and requires that a member purchase stock in the fund for membership. The CLF obtains its funding through credit union capital investments and borrowings from the Federal Financing Bank, which provides reduced-cost financing to federal agencies that issue government-backed obligations.

GAO-12-247 National Credit Union Administration

indirectly through a corporate, which acts as an agent for its members. U.S. Central was the primary agent for the CLF and was the depository for CLF funds until August 2009, when NCUA changed its investment strategy for the liquidity facility.

NCUA Supervision and Examination of the Corporates and Credit Unions

NCUA supervises and issues regulations on operations and services for federally chartered credit unions and for both state- and federally chartered corporates.[20] NCUA has supervisory and regulatory authority over both state- and federally chartered corporates because they provide services to federally insured credit unions. In addition, NCUA shares responsibility for overseeing state-chartered credit unions to help ensure they pose no risk to the insurance fund.[21]

To supervise federally chartered credit unions and corporates, NCUA conducts on-site examinations and off-site monitoring of credit union call report data and other financial information that credit unions report on a regular basis. In 2008, NCUA changed its on-site examination schedule for credit unions from a risked-based scheduling program that required two examinations every 3 years to a 12-month cycle. For corporates, NCUA conducts annual on-site examinations and reviews call report data and operational trends. Also, on-site NCUA examiners and capital markets specialists may be assigned on a full-time basis at a corporate.[22] For state-chartered credit unions, NCUA relies on state supervisory

---

[20]Part 704 of NCUA's regulations, together with the relevant provisions of the Federal Credit Union Act of 1934, constitute the primary federal regulatory framework for both state- and federally chartered corporates. NCUA's Office of Corporate Credit Unions is responsible for supervising corporate credit unions and U.S. Central. NCUA's regulations (C.F.R. 12, Part 700 through 761), together with the relevant provisions of the Federal Credit Union Act of 1934, constitute the primary federal regulatory framework for both state- and federally chartered credit unions.

[21]State supervisory agencies supervise state-chartered credit unions and issue regulations on field of membership and scope of services.

[22]NCUA categorizes corporate supervision into three categories (Types I, II, and III) based on asset size, investment authorities, complexity of operations, and influence on the market or credit union system. For example, a corporate with Type III supervision generally has billions of dollars in assets, exercises expanded investment authorities, maintains complex and innovative operations, and has a significant impact in the marketplace and on the credit union system. NCUA assigns a full-time, on-site examiner to corporates with Type III supervision.

GAO-12-247 National Credit Union Administration

agency examinations, performs off-site monitoring, and conducts joint examinations of credit unions with state supervisory agencies.

As part of its on-site examinations, NCUA assesses a credit union's exposure to risk and assigns risk-weighted ratings under the CAMEL rating system. The ratings reflect a credit union's condition in five components: capital adequacy, asset quality, management, earnings, and liquidity. Each component is rated on a scale of 1 to 5, with 1 being the best and 5 the worst. The five component ratings are then used to develop a single composite rating, also ranging from 1 to 5. Credit unions with composite ratings of 1 or 2 are considered to be in satisfactory condition, while credit unions with composite ratings of 3, 4, or 5 exhibit varying levels of safety and soundness problems. A similar rating system, known as the Corporate Risk Information System, is used to assess the corporates.

NCUA has the authority to take an enforcement action against credit unions and corporates to correct deficiencies identified during an examination or as a result of off-site monitoring. NCUA can issue letters of understanding and agreement, which is an agreement between NCUA and the credit union or corporate on certain steps the credit union or corporate will take to correct deficiencies. They can also issue preliminary warning letters, which is an NCUA directive to a credit union or corporate to take certain actions to correct deficiencies. Further, NCUA can issue a cease-and-desist order, which requires a credit union or corporate to take action to correct deficiencies. Although not considered an enforcement action, NCUA examiners also can issue documents of resolution to record NCUA's direction that a credit union or corporate take certain action to correct a deficiency or issue within a specified period.

NCUA also has a number of options for dealing with a credit union or corporate that has severe deficiencies or is insolvent. It can place the institution into conservatorship—that is, NCUA takes over the credit union's or corporates' operations. After NCUA assumes control of the institution's operations, it determines whether the credit union or corporate can continue operating as a viable entity. To resolve a credit union or corporate that is insolvent or no longer viable, NCUA may merge it with or without assistance, conduct a purchase and assumption, or liquidate its assets. In an assisted merger, a stronger credit union or corporate assumes all the assets and liabilities of the failed credit union or corporate with NCUA providing financial incentives or an asset guarantee. In a purchase and assumption, another credit union or corporate purchases specific assets and assumes specific liabilities of the failed corporate or credit union. In liquidation, NCUA sells the assets of a failed credit union or corporate.

PCA Framework

PCA is a comprehensive framework of mandatory and discretionary supervisory actions for credit unions.[23] PCA is based on five categories and their associated net worth ratios—that is, capital as a percentage of assets (see table 1). If a credit union falls below well capitalized (7 percent net worth), the credit union is required to increase retained earnings.[24] When NCUA determines the credit union is in the undercapitalized, significantly undercapitalized, or critically undercapitalized categories, NCUA is required to take additional mandatory supervisory actions. In addition to these mandatory supervisory actions, NCUA often enforces discretionary supervisory actions. Discretionary supervisory actions are applied to credit unions that fall into the undercapitalized category or below and include requiring NCUA approval for acquisitions or new lines of business, restricting dividends paid to members, and dismissing the credit union's board members or senior management.

[23]Credit unions that have been in operation for less than 10 years and have $10 million or less in total assets are governed by an alternate set of PCA provisions, as provided by Section 216 of the Federal Credit Union Act. Also see 12 C.F.R. § 702, 301 et seq.

[24]An earnings retention requires a credit union that is adequately capitalized or lower to increase the dollar amount of its net worth quarterly by at least 0.1 percent of its total assets by transferring that amount from undivided earnings to its regular reserve account until it is "well capitalized."

GAO-12-247 National Credit Union Administration

Table 1: PCA Categories for Credit Unions, effective February 2000

Category	Net worth ratio (capital as a percentage of assets)	Mandatory supervisory actions
Well-capitalized	7% or greater	None
Adequately capitalized	6 to 6.99	Earnings retention
Undercapitalized	4 to 5.99	• Earnings retention
Significantly undercapitalized	2 to 3.99	• Submission of an acceptable net worth restoration plan • Restriction on asset growth • Restriction on member business lending
Critically undercapitalized	less than 2	• Earnings retention • Submission of an acceptable net worth restoration plan • Restriction on asset growth • Restriction on member business lending • NCUA must place the credit union in liquidation, conservatorship or take other corrective action

Source: GAO analysis of NCUA regulations.

Note: Significantly undercapitalized also includes a credit union with a net worth ratio of less than 5 percent if that credit union fails to submit an acceptable net worth restoration plan within the allotted time or materially fails to implement the net worth restoration plan.

Before 2010, U.S. Central and other corporate credit unions were not subject to PCA but were instead required to maintain total capital at a minimum of 4 percent of their moving daily average net assets. Total capital for U.S. Central and corporate credit unions was calculated using any combination of retained earnings, paid-in capital, or membership capital. If total capital fell below this level, NCUA required U.S. Central or the corporate to submit a capital restoration plan. If the capital restoration plan was inadequate or the corporate failed to complete the plan, NCUA could issue a capital directive. A capital directive orders the corporate to take a variety of actions including reducing dividends, ending or limiting lending of certain loan categories, ending or limiting the purchase of investments, and limiting operational expenses in order to achieve adequate capitalization within a specified time frame.

Corporate and Credit Union Failures Were Largely the Result of Poor Investment Strategies and Weak Management

From January 1, 2008, to June 30, 2011, 5 corporates and 85 credit unions failed.[25] The five failed corporates—U.S. Central, Western Corporate (Wescorp), Members United, Southwest, and Constitution—were some of the largest institutions within the corporate system, although the credit unions that failed were relatively small. Specifically, these five failed corporates accounted for 75 percent of all corporate assets as of December 31, 2007 (see fig. 2). In contrast, the 85 credit unions that eventually failed represented around 1 percent of all credit unions and less than 1 percent of total credit union assets, as of December 31, 2007.

Figure 2: Assets of Corporate Credit Unions, as of December 31, 2007

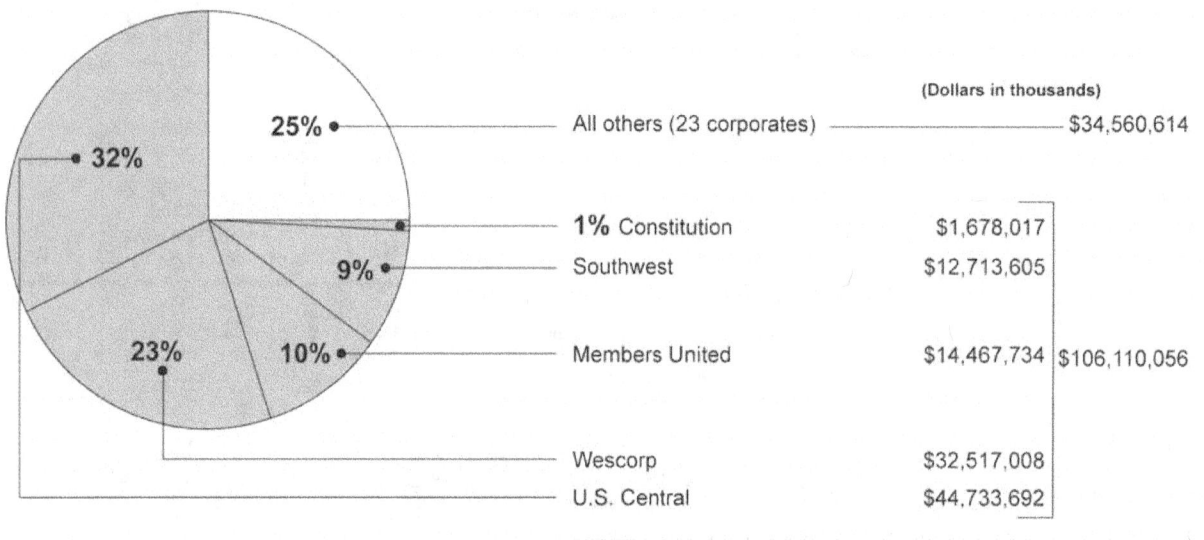

(Dollars in thousands)

All others (23 corporates)	$34,560,614
1% Constitution	$1,678,017
Southwest	$12,713,605
Members United	$14,467,734
Wescorp	$32,517,008
U.S. Central	$44,733,692

$106,110,056

$140,670,670

U.S. Central and failed corporates

Source: GAO analysis of SNL Financial data.

---

[25]For the purpose of our analysis, a failed corporate or credit union is defined as a credit union that is no longer viable or insolvent and resolved with NCUA assistance. This includes NCUA's assistance with mergers, purchases and assumptions and involuntary liquidations.

GAO-12-247 National Credit Union Administration

Poor Investment and Business Strategies Contributed to Corporate Failures

NCUA's OIG MLRs of the failed corporates and our analysis of historical financial data for the corporate system show that management of both U.S. Central and the failed corporate credit unions made poor investment decisions. Specifically, U.S. Central and the failed corporates overconcentrated their investments in private-label, mortgage-backed securities (MBS), investing substantially more in private-label MBS than corporate credit unions that did not fail (see fig. 3).[26] At the end of 2007, the five failed corporates had invested 31 to 74 percent of their assets in private-label MBS. In particular, Wescorp and U.S. Central had invested 74 percent and 49 percent, respectively, of their portfolio in private-label MBS. In contrast, 10 of the 23 remaining corporates had also invested in private-label MBS but at lower levels—for example, from 1 to 19 percent.[27] These high concentrations of private-label MBS exposed the failed corporates to the highs and lows of the real estate market, which experienced significant losses.

---

[26]Private-label MBS include mortgages such as subprime and Alt-A mortgages (those mortgages with borrowers whose risk profiles fall between prime loans and subprime loans) that were pooled and then securitized by entities other than the government-sponsored enterprises. About 75 percent of subprime and Alt-A mortgages originated from 2001 through 2007 were securitized. Since 2007, the rise in mortgage delinquencies and foreclosures has been particularly acute in this segment of the mortgage market. For more information, see GAO, *Nonprime Mortgages: Analysis of Loan Performance, Factors Associated with Defaults, and Data Sources*, GAO-10-805 (Washington, D.C.: Aug. 24, 2010).

[27]Corporates typically have a high rate of investments as a percentage of assets. For example, at the end of 2007, on average corporates had approximately 90 percent of their total assets invested.

Figure 3: Percentages of Private-Label MBS Held by U.S. Central and Corporates, from 2003 through 2008

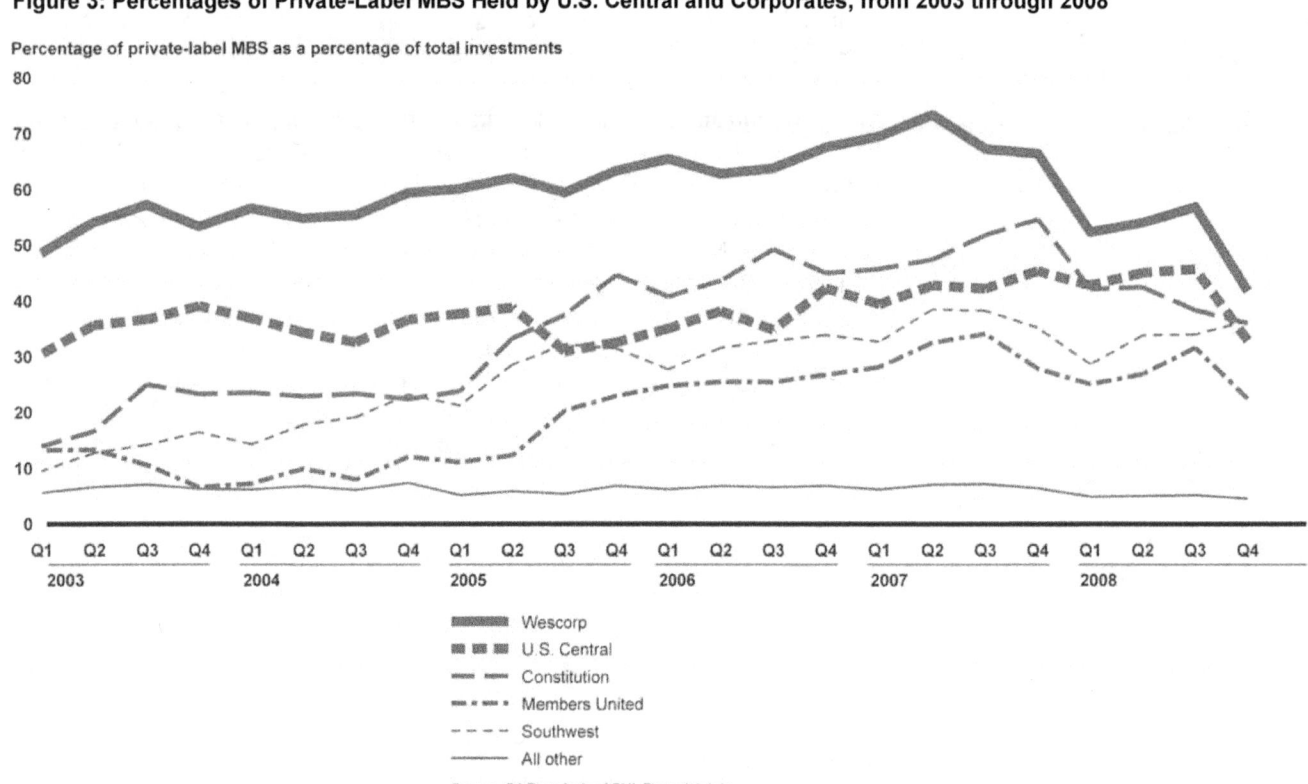

Percentage of private-label MBS as a percentage of total investments

Source: GAO analysis of SNL Financial data.

Furthermore, corporates had significant deposits in U.S. Central, which led to indirect exposure to its high concentration of private-label MBS and losses when it failed. For example, in 2007, Members United had invested more than 40 percent of total assets in U.S. Central, and Southwest and Constitution had each invested approximately 30 percent of total assets, according to the MLRs.

In addition to poor investment decisions, the business strategies U.S. Central and the other four failed corporates' pursued contributed to their failure. Specifically, their management implemented business strategies to attract and retain credit union members by offering lower rates on services and higher returns on investments. According to the MLRs, U.S. Central shifted towards an aggressive growth strategy to maintain and increase its market share of corporates. This strategy led its management to increase its holdings of high-yielding investments, including private-label MBS. From 2006 to 2007, U.S. Central's assets grew by 22 percent as members invested their liquid funds in return for competitive rates. The other failed corporates implemented similar business strategies.

The financial crisis exposed the problems in the corporates' investment and business strategies, leading to a severe liquidity crisis within the credit union system. Specifically, the downturn severely diminished the value and market for private-label MBS and depositors lost confidence in the corporate system because of the institutions' substantial investment in these securities. The decline in value of these investments resulted in corporates borrowing significant amounts of short-term funds from outside of the credit union system to meet liquidity needs as credit unions reduced their deposits. However, these options became limited when credit rating agencies and lenders lost confidence in individual corporates and some lines of credit were suspended. For example, from 2007 to 2009, credit rating agencies downgraded U.S. Central's long- and short-term credit ratings, and in 2009, the Federal Reserve Bank of Kansas City downgraded its borrowing ability.[28] Eventually, the deterioration of the underlying credit quality of the private-label MBS led to the corporates' insolvencies.

Poor Management Was the Primary Reason That 85 Credit Unions Failed

According to our analysis of NCUA's and its OIG's data, the 85 credit union failures were primarily the result of poor management.[29] Management of failed credit unions exposed their institutions to increased operational, credit, liquidity, and concentration risks, which it then failed to properly monitor or mitigate. The following describes these risks and provides examples of how exposure to these risks led to the failure of a number of credit unions.

Operational risk includes the risk of loss due to inadequate or failed internal controls, due diligence, and oversight. We found that management's failure to control operational risk contributed to 76 of the 85 failures. For example, Norlarco Credit Union's management had weak

---

[28]U.S. Central had a line of credit with the Federal Reserve Bank of Kansas prior to the financial crisis.

[29]To conduct this analysis we reviewed NCUA regional examiner reports for all of the failed credit unions and postmortem reports, which were conducted on 15 of the 85 failed credit unions. In addition, we reviewed the NCUA OIG's MLRs for 10 of the 85 failed credit unions and information in the OIG's Semiannual Report to the Congress for April 1, 2010, to September 30, 2010, and October 1, 2010, to March 31, 2011.

oversight policies and controls for an out of state construction lending program and failed to perform due diligence before entering into a relationship with a third party responsible for managing it. Norlarco's management allowed the third party to have complete control in making and overseeing all of the credit union's residential construction loans, leading to a decline in borrower credit quality and underreported delinquencies. Potential losses from its residential construction loan program led to Norlarco's insolvency.

Management's failure to control operational risk can also create the potential for fraud. We analyzed NCUA's and its OIG's data and found that fraud or alleged fraud at credit unions contributed to 29 of 85 of credit union failures. According to NCUA, credit unions with inadequate internal controls are susceptible to fraud. In addition, NCUA's internal assessments of fraud showed that their examiners often had cited inactive boards or Supervisory Committees, limited number of staff, and poor record keeping before the fraud was discovered at the failed credit unions. For example, the OIG reported that Certified Federal Credit Union's internal controls were severely lacking, enabling the chief executive officer to report erroneous financial results to the credit union's board and in quarterly call reports. According to the MLR, before the fraud was identified, the credit union's board was weak and unresponsive to repeated reports of inaccurate accounting records and weak internal controls from NCUA examiners and external auditors. The credit union was involuntarily liquidated in 2010. NCUA OIG officials told us that some other indicators of potential fraud are high ratios of investments to assets and a low number of loan delinquencies.

Credit risk is the possibility that a borrower will not repay a loan or will default. We found that management's failure to control for credit risk contributed to 58 of the 85 credit union failures. For example, Clearstar Financial Credit Union management originated and funded a significant number of loans that were poorly underwritten—that is, they were made to borrowers with poor credit histories. Management then compounded these mistakes by extending delinquent loans and poor collection practices, contributing to the credit union's eventual failure.

Moreover, management at some failed credit unions did not consistently monitor the credit risk associated with member business loans (MBL). With some limitations, credit unions can lend to their members for business purposes.[30] However, these loans can be risky for credit unions. For example, NCUA reported in recent congressional testimony that due to the lack of credit union expertise and challenging macroeconomic conditions, over half of the losses sustained by the NCUSIF were related to MBLs for a two year period in the late 1980s.[31] Our analysis of NCUA's and its OIG's data indicated that MBLs contributed to 13 of the 85 credit union failures. According to our analysis of historical financial data, failed credit unions had more MBLs as a percentage of assets than peer credit unions that did not fail or the credit union industry (see fig. 4).[32] In addition, more than 40 percent of failed credit unions participated in member business lending. Comparatively, NCUA had testified that only 30 percent of all credit unions participated in member business lending, as of March 31, 2011.

---

[30]Most credit unions are restricted from lending more than 12.25 percent of assets as MBLs. Recently there have been congressional proposals to raise the cap to 27.5 percent. The majority of MBLs, $31.4 billion, or 84 percent, are secured by real estate. Agricultural-related MBLs have steadily grown to $1.4 billion, representing approximately 4 percent of total MBLs. More than one-third of all MBLs ($14 billion) are held by credit unions in three states. California credit unions account for the largest percentage of total MBLs (20 percent, or $7.5 billion), followed by New York credit unions (11 percent, or $4.2 billion), then Wisconsin credit unions (6 percent, or $2.3 billion).

[31]See NCUA, *Statement of the Honorable Debbie Matz, Chairman National Credit Union Administration "Credit Unions: Member Business Lending" Before the Senate Committee on Banking, Housing, and Urban Affairs* (June 16, 2011).

[32]We reviewed financial filings from the fourth quarter of 2005 through the third quarter of 2010 for three groups: (1) the 85 credit unions that failed from January 2008 to June 2011; (2) a group of 340 peer credit unions—the four closest credit unions in terms of assets within the state as each failed credit union; and (3) the broader industry to include all credit unions that reported for each quarter within the period.

Figure 4: MBLs as a Percentage of Total Assets, December 31, 2005, to September 30, 2010

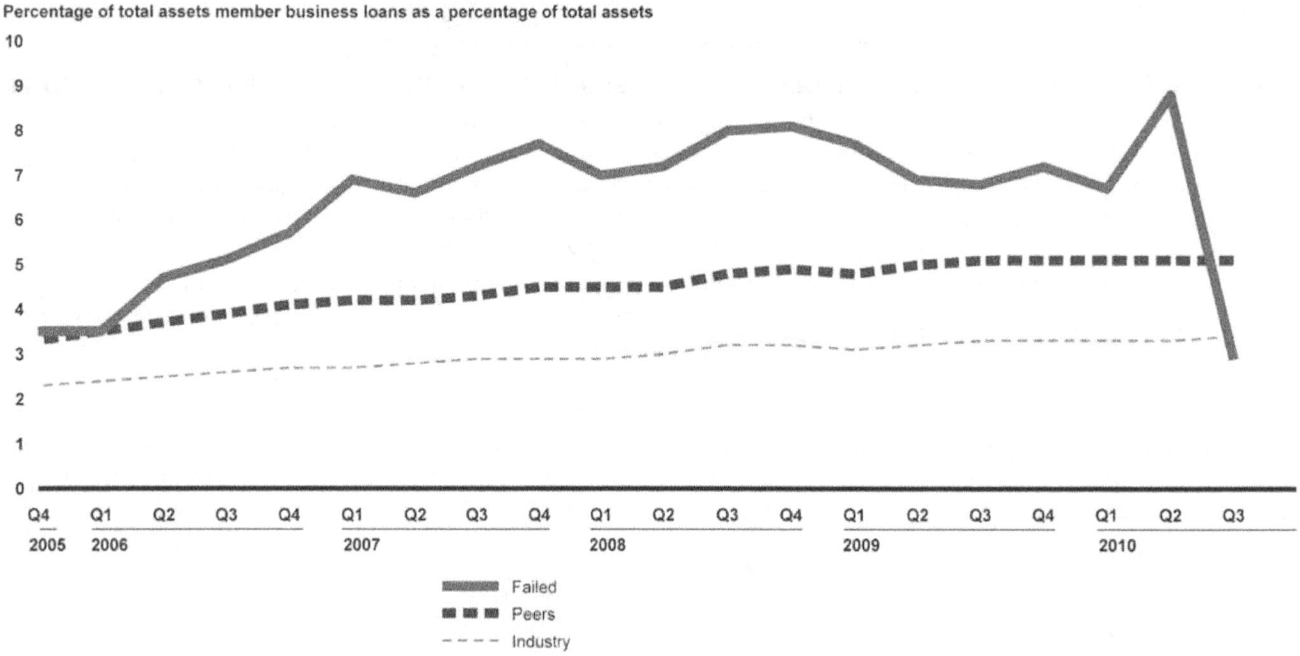

Percentage of total assets member business loans as a percentage of total assets

Failed
Peers
Industry

Source: GAO analysis of SNL Financial data.

Liquidity risk is the risk that the credit union may not be able to meet expenses or cover member withdrawals because of illiquid assets. We found that liquidity risk contributed to 31 of the 85 credit union failures. For example, the management of Ensign Federal Credit Union relied on a $12 million deposit to fund credit union operations. However, when the deposit was withdrawn in 2009, the credit union lacked other funding sources to meet normal member demands and operational expenses, contributing to the credit union's failure.

Concentration risk is excessive exposure to certain markets, industries, or groups. While some level of concentration may not be avoidable, it is the responsibility of management to put in place appropriate controls, policies, and systems to monitor the associated risks. We found that concentration risk contributed to 27 of the 85 credit union failures. For example, High Desert Federal Credit Union's management began expanding its real estate construction lending in 2003, and by 2006, its loan portfolio had more than doubled from $73 million to $154 million. In 2006, construction lending accounted for more than 60 percent of the credit union's loan portfolio. When the housing market collapsed, its concentration in the real estate construction loans led to its insolvency.

OIG Identified Weaknesses in NCUA's Examination Processes for Corporates and Credit Unions

In addition to the management weaknesses in corporates and credit unions, NCUA's examination and enforcement processes did not result in strong and timely actions to avert the failure of these institutions. The OIG found that stronger and timelier action on the part of NCUA could have reduced losses from the failures from U.S. Central and the four other failed corporates. NCUA examiners had observed the substantial concentration of private-label MBS for U.S Central and three of the four other corporates that failed prior to 2008, but did not take timely action to address these concentrations. For example, NCUA examiners observed Wescorp's growing concentration in private-label MBS beginning in 2003; but they did not limit or take action to address this issue until 2008. Similarly, the OIG's material loss review of Southwest Corporate cites that NCUA's March 2008 exam concluded, "current and allowable MBS exposures are significant given the unprecedented market dislocation... Southwest's exposure is clearly excessive." However, the MLR did not indicate that NCUA issued a document of resolution or enforcement action to address Southwest's high concentration. In the case of Constitution Corporate, the MLR noted that NCUA took enforcement action to address concentration limits prior to failure.

Similar to its findings for corporate failures, the OIG found weaknesses in NCUA's examination and enforcement processes for 10 of the 11 failed credit unions for which it conducted MLRs. In particular, the OIG stated that "if examiners acted more aggressively in their supervision actions, the looming safety and soundness concerns that were present early-on in nearly every failed institution, could have been identified sooner and the eventual losses to the NCUSIF could have been stopped or mitigated."

The OIG made a number of recommendations to address the problems that the financial crisis exposed.[33] For example, to better ensure that corporate credit unions set prudent concentration limits, the OIG recommended that NCUA provide corporate credit unions with more definitive guidance on limiting investment portfolio concentrations. Based

---

[33]The OIG conducted individual MLRs on U.S. Central and the four failed corporates and based on these reviews made six recommendations to NCUA. See www.ncua.gov, accessed January 3, 2012.

on the credit union failures, the OIG recommended that NCUA take steps to strengthen their examinations process by, among other things, improving the review of call reports and third-party relationships, as well as following up credit union actions in response to documents of resolution and the quality control review process for examinations. Appendix I contains more information on the status of NCUA's implementation of OIG's recommendations.

NCUA Has Taken Various Actions to Stabilize and Reform the Corporate System

NCUA took actions to stabilize, resolve, and reform the corporate system and to minimize the costs of its intervention. NCUA based these actions on four guiding principles:

- to avoid any interruption of services provided by corporate credit unions to credit unions;

- to prevent a run on corporate shares by maintaining confidence in the overall credit union system;

- to facilitate a corporate resolution process in line with sound public policy that is at the least possible cost to the credit unions over the long term, while avoiding moral hazard; and

- to reform the credit union system through new corporate rules with a revised corporate and regulatory structure.

NCUA established a number of measures to ensure that corporates had access to liquidity. To resolve the failed corporates, NCUA placed five corporates—U.S. Central, Wescorp, Members United, Southwest, and Constitution—into conservatorship and isolated their nonperforming assets. To reform the system, NCUA enacted new rules to address the causes of the failures, assessed credit unions for corporate losses, forecasted the impact of future assessments through scenario tests, and took measures to reduce moral hazard. Through these actions, NCUA attempted to resolve the corporates' losses at the least possible cost. However, we could not verify all NCUA's estimated losses of the corporates' and credit union failures.

NCUA Used Existing and Temporary Funding Sources to Stabilize the Corporate System

To provide liquidity, NCUA used two existing funds—NCUSIF and CLF—and based on legislative changes, created a temporary fund—the Temporary Corporate Credit Union Stabilization Fund (Stabilization Fund). NCUA also created four new programs—the Credit Union System Investment Program (CU-SIP), the Credit Union Homeowners' Affordability Relief Program (CU-HARP), the Temporary Corporate Credit Union Liquidity Guarantee Program (Liquidity Guarantee Program), and the Temporary Corporate Credit Union Share Guarantee Program (Share Guarantee Program). See appendix III for more information about these programs.

NCUA used NCUSIF to provide liquidity to the corporate system. As stated earlier, U.S. Central had experienced substantial losses, impairing its ability to provide liquidity to the credit union system. In December 2008, NCUA provided for a NCUSIF loan to U.S. Central to cover an end-of-year liquidity shortfall. The loan was outstanding for 3 days and then fully repaid. In January 2009, NCUA placed a $1 billion capital note in U.S. Central.[34] NCUSIF subsequently wrote off this note when it determined the credit losses on the private label MBS (held by U.S. Central) impaired the full value of the note.

NCUA also borrowed from the CLF, one of its primary liquidity facilities for the credit union system. Prior to the 2007-2009 financial crisis, the obligation limit on the CLF's borrowing authority with Treasury was $1.5 billion. At NCUA's request, Congress removed the appropriation limit in 2008 allowing CLF to borrow up to its full legal borrowing authority.[35] Under the formula in the Federal Credit Union Act, CLF could borrow up to $41 billion at that time. In March 2009, CLF borrowed $10 billion from the Federal Financing Bank and lent it to NCUSIF.[36] Because the CLF is

---

[34]A capital note is a short-term debt issuance that is usually not collateralized.

[35]To avoid compromising its borrowing authority with Treasury, NCUA changed the CLF's investment strategy in mid-2009. Specifically, before 2009, the CLF's funds from subscribed capital stock and retained earnings placed in a deposit account with U.S. Central, the CLF agent. However, given U.S. Central's insolvency, NCUA moved its funds out of U.S. Central and invested them with Treasury in 2009, to avoid an adverse accounting treatment for the fund—thereby reducing the fund's member equity and ultimately limiting its borrowing authority with Treasury.

[36]As discussed earlier, the Federal Financing Bank is administered by Treasury and provides reduced-cost financing to federal agencies that issue government-backed obligations.

restricted from lending directly to corporates, NCUA then used funds from NCUSIF to lend $5 billion to U.S. Central and $5 billion to Wescorp. By October 2010, U.S. Central and Wescorp had repaid their loans to NCUSIF using funds raised primarily from the sale of more than $10 billion in unencumbered marketable securities that sold near their par value in August and September 2010.[37] NCUA subsequently repaid its $10 billion CLF loan with proceeds from asset sales.

In addition, NCUA used a temporary fund created by Congress in 2009 to help increase liquidity in the system. In May 2009, Congress passed the Helping Families Save Their Homes Act, which, among other things, created a temporary fund to absorb losses from corporates.[38] In particular, the act created the Stabilization Fund, which replaced NCUSIF as the primary source to absorb the corporates' losses. The act also amended the Federal Credit Union Act to give NCUA the authority to levy assessments over the life of the Stabilization Fund to repay the corporates' losses instead of repaying them in a lump sum.[39] In addition, it increased NCUA's borrowing authority with Treasury up to $6 billion through a revolving loan fund to be shared between the Stabilization Fund and NCUSIF.[40]

To increase liquidity for the corporates, NCUA also established four programs,

- *CU-SIP and CU-HARP.* In early 2009, NCUA established these programs to provide a temporary source of stable funding to the corporates. Due to the restriction preventing the CLF from lending directly to the corporates, NCUA designed both programs so that the CLF would lend to the credit unions, which then purchased notes issued by corporates.[41] The corporates were then required to use the

---

[37]Once NCUA was prepared to liquidate the corporates, it began the process of unwinding—that is, closing out—derivatives contracts and other arrangements that encumbered these securities, freeing them up to be sold.

[38]Amending the Federal Credit Union Act, 12 U.S.C. §§ 1751-1795k.

[39]The assessment period was initially a 7-year period and was changed after the Stabilization Fund was extended to 2021.

[40]As mentioned earlier, the act also extended the temporary increase in members' share insurance amount with NCUSIF from $100,000 to $250,000 to increase confidence in the credit union system and prevent a run on member shares.

[41]The corporates used CU-SIP/CU-HARP funds to repay outstanding collateralized debt to protect their interests in the collateral.

funds to pay down their external debt, freeing up assets that had been posted as collateral against the debt. In exchange for participating in the programs, the corporates were required to pay CLF borrowing costs to credit unions and an additional fee to the credit unions as an incentive for them to participate in the programs. CLF lending to credit unions totaled approximately $8.2 billion under CU-SIP and about $164 million under CU-HARP. All borrowings for both programs were repaid in 2010.

- *Liquidity Guarantee Program and Share Guarantee Program.* NCUA created these two temporary guarantee programs in late 2008 and early 2009 to help stabilize confidence and dissuade withdrawals by credit unions, in an attempt to avoid a run on the corporates. These programs provided temporary guarantees on certain new unsecured debt obligations issued by eligible corporates and credit union shares held in corporates in excess of $250,000. Initially, NCUA provided the coverage to all the corporates for a limited time but later provided extensions to continue guaranteeing coverage to corporates that did not opt out of the program. Based on NCUA's 2009 financial statements, no guarantee payments were required for either program. However, as of December 19, 2011, the audited financial statements for calendar year 2010 of the Stabilization Fund were not completed and available.

NCUA Took Steps to Resolve Corporate Failures and Maintain Ongoing Payment System Functions

NCUA took a variety of steps to resolve the failed corporates and maintain corporate payment processing services for credit unions. First, in April 2009, NCUA enacted a temporary waiver to allow corporates not meeting their minimum capital requirements to continue to provide services to credit unions. In particular, the waiver allowed corporates to use their capital levels of record on their November 2008 call reports in order to continue providing the necessary core operational services to credit unions. In addition, it granted the Office of Corporate Credit Unions discretionary authority to modify or restrict the use of this capital waiver for certain corporates based on safety and soundness considerations. Without the waiver, corporates that failed to meet the minimum capital requirements would have had to cease or significantly curtail operations, including payment system services and lending and borrowing activities. As a result, the credit union system would have faced substantial interruptions in its daily operations, potentially leading to a loss of confidence in other parts of the financial system.

Second, NCUA ultimately placed the five failing corporates into conservatorship.[42] According to NCUA, it placed the corporates into conservatorships to reduce systemic exposure, exert greater direct control, improve the transparency of financial information, minimize cost, maintain confidence, and continue payment system processing. When placing the five corporates into conservatorship, NCUA replaced the corporates' existing boards, the chief executive officers, and in some cases, the management teams and took over operations to resolve the corporates in an orderly manner. As a part of the conservatorships, NCUA set up bridge institutions for the wholesale corporate—U.S. Central—and the three other corporates.[43] Through these bridge institutions, NCUA managed the corporates' illiquid assets and maintained payment services to the member credit unions.[44] The member credit unions must provide sufficient capital to acquire the operations of these bridge institutions from NCUA.[45]

Third, NCUA established a securitization program to provide long-term funding for the legacy assets formerly held in the securities portfolios of certain corporate credit unions by issuing NCUA-guaranteed notes. NCUA's analysis showed that MBS were trading at market prices considerably below the intrinsic value that would eventually be received by long-term investors.[46] NCUA used a method similar to the "good bank-

---

[42]In March 2009, NCUA placed U.S. Central and Wescorp into conservatorship. In September 2010, NCUA placed Constitution, Members United, and Southwest into conservatorships.

[43]Bridge institutions are temporary institutions chartered by NCUA for the purpose of continuing services to member credit unions during a transition period. These institutions remain under NCUA authority while member credit unions determine their long-term service options, perform appropriate due diligence, and implement the necessary operational changes.

[44]After conservatorship, NCUA merged Constitution Corporate into Member's United Bridge. Therefore, NCUA created four bridge institutions for the conserved corporates.

[45]As of October 30, 2011, two of the four bridge institutions—Members United Bridge and Southwest Bridge—had been acquired by newly chartered institutions. Former members of Members United Bridge are now served by Alloya Corporate and members of Southwest Bridge by Catalyst Corporate.

[46]Prior to obtaining long-term funding, NCUA considered funding the corporate credit unions' bad assets with borrowings from Treasury. However, NCUA determined that it was more beneficial to have collateral up front by securitizing the assets and avoid reducing its borrowing authority with Treasury if needed later.

bad bank" model that the Federal Deposit Insurance Corporation has sometimes adopted with insolvent banks to remove illiquid or "bad" assets from the failed corporates. In particular, NCUA transferred the corporates' assets into Asset Management Estates, also known as liquidation estates.[47] Using these estates, NCUA held and isolated the corporates' illiquid assets (i.e., MBS) from the bridge institutions and issued the NCUA-guaranteed notes.

NCUA issued $28 billion (at the point of securitization) in these NCUA-guaranteed notes, while the face value of the original MBS assets was approximately $50 billion.[48] NCUA structured each of the guaranteed notes so that its value would approximate the value of the principal and interest cash flows on the underlying legacy assets. NCUA officials said that by structuring the notes in this manner, NCUA minimized its exposure in the event that the underlying cash flow was less than the notes' value. According to NCUA's term sheet, cash flows from the underlying securities will be used to make principal and interest payments to holders of the notes, and NCUA guarantees timely payments. NCUA issued 13 separate notes, with the final sales occurring in June 2011 and maturing between 2017 and 2021. Any necessary guarantee payments are to be made from the Stabilization Fund, which also expires in 2021.

Finally, as of November 2011, NCUA has initiated lawsuits against parties it believes are liable for the corporates' MBS-related losses. These lawsuits allege violations of federal and state securities laws and misrepresentations in the sale of hundreds of securities, according to NCUA.[49]

---

[47]NCUA established these estates through its Asset Management Assistance Center, which has the authority to oversee the funding and disposal of bad assets.

[48]NCUA relied on external consultants—in addition to its own analysis—to estimate its losses from the failed corporate credit unions.

[49]If successful, any proceeds would be returned to the Stabilization Fund.

NCUA Enacted Rules to Address the Causes of Corporate Failures

NCUA issued a new rule for corporates to address the key causes of the failures.[50] Among other things, the rule (1) eliminates the definition and separate treatment of the wholesale corporate or third tier of the credit union system, (2) prohibits corporates from investing in certain securities and set sector concentration limits, (3) creates a new system of capital standards and PCA for corporates, and (4) introduces new corporate governance requirements. Some parts of the new rule addresses the recommendations of NCUA's OIG. NCUA issued the rule on October 20, 2010, and it will be implemented over a number of years. For additional information on the rule, see appendix IV.

- *Essentially eliminate the wholesale corporate or third tier of the credit union system.* The new corporate rule that NCUA issued on October 20, 2010, eliminated both the definition of and the requirements applicable to a wholesale corporate or the third tier of the credit union system.[51] NCUA essentially eliminated the wholesale corporate, in part, to mitigate inefficiency and systemic risk in the credit union system. The failure of U.S. Central, the credit union system's only wholesale corporate, highlights some of the risks. Specifically, its failure contributed to the failure of three corporates, instability in the other corporates, and substantial losses to the Stabilization Fund.

- *Prohibit corporates from certain investments and set sector concentration limits.* NCUA amended the corporate rule to prohibit certain investments, such as private-label MBS, and set certain sector concentration limits.[52] In addition to prohibiting private-label MBS, the rule prohibits corporate investments in collateralized-debt obligations, net interest-margin securities, and subordinated securities. Previously, corporates were allowed to set their own sector concentration limits, which enabled them to continually increase their limits or set excessive limits. The new rule sets maximum sector concentration limits for corporate investments and addresses OIG recommendations that NCUA provide corporates with more definitive guidance on

---

[50]NCUA published a proposed rule in December 2009 with the public comment period ending March 2010.

[51]The rule was effective January 18, 2011, except for specified provisions.

[52]The new investment, credit risk and asset-liability management provisions generally took effect 90 days after publication of the final rule (i.e., Jan. 18, 2011). A corporate holding investments that violate the new prohibitions must submit an investment action plan to NCUA under 12 C.F.R. § 704.10.

limiting investment portfolio concentrations. Corporates are limited to investing less than 1,000 percent of capital or 50 percent of total assets in specific investments, including agency MBS, corporate debt obligations, municipal securities, and government-guaranteed student loan asset-backed securities.[53] Furthermore, corporates are restricted from investing more than 500 percent of capital or 25 percent of total assets in other asset-backed security sectors, including auto loans and leases, private-label student loans, credit card loans, or any sector not explicitly noted in the rules. NCUA has taken additional steps to mitigate the associated risk by limiting the weighted-average life of the portfolio to approximately 2 years. NCUA also tightened the limits on securities purchased from a single obligor from 50 percent of capital to 25 percent.

- *Create a new system of capital standards and PCA for corporates.* NCUA's new corporate rule also established a revised set of capital standards for corporates and PCA framework. The new capital standards replace the existing 4 percent mandatory minimum capital requirement with three minimum capital ratios, including two risk-based capital ratios and a leverage ratio (see table 2).[54] The risk-based capital and interim leverage ratios became enforceable on October 20, 2011, and all corporates were required to meet these capital standards.[55] Starting in October 2011, corporates are also subject to PCA if their capital falls below the adequately capitalized level for any of the three capital ratios. As discussed earlier, a corporate becomes subject to more severe supervisory actions and restrictions on its activities if its capital continues to fall.

---

[53]Agency MBS are government-guaranteed MBS, which differ from private-label MBS because they are originated or securitized by a government-sponsored enterprise or government agency. The concentration limit on real-estate MBS is set at no more than 300 percent of capital or 15 percent of assets for commercial MBS.

[54]See the preamble to the final rule, at 75 Fed. Reg. 64789-64792 and 64794-64802, for background on the new capital standards. The new capital standards initially took partial effect 1 year after publication of the rule (i.e., Oct. 20, 2011) and are then phased in during the next 10 years.

[55]The leverage ratio evolves over time, reducing the amount of contributed capital that qualifies for inclusion in the leverage ratio. The amount of retained earnings included in the leverage ratio becomes effective in 2013 and is fully phased in by 2020.

Table 2: Corporate Capital and PCA Standards, as of October 2011

Categories	Total risk based capital ratio	Tier-one risk based capital ratio	Leverage ratio
Well Capitalized	10%	6%	5%
Adequately capitalized	8	4	4
Undercapitalized	Less than 8	Less than 4	Less than 4
Significantly undercapitalized	Less than 6	Less than 3	Less than 3
Critically undercapitalized	Less than 4	Less than 2	Less than 2

Source: GAO analysis of NCUA regulations.

Note: In addition to meeting required capital standards a corporate must not be subject to any written agreement, order, capital directive, or PCA directive issued by NCUA to meet a specific capital level for any capital measure.

- *Introduce new corporate governance requirements.* NCUA has instituted a new corporate governance rule. To ensure that corporate board members have adequate knowledge and experience to oversee sophisticated corporate investment and operation strategies, they must hold an executive management position, such as chief executive offer, chief financial officer, or chief operating officer of a credit union.[56] Corporate board members are also prohibited from serving on more than one corporate credit union board. According to NCUA, this restriction will help ensure that board members' loyalty is undivided and that they are not distracted by competing demands from another corporate. Effective October 21, 2013, the majority of a corporate's board members must be representatives from member credit unions. The purpose of this rule is to limit another corporate from serving other corporates rather than serving their member credit unions. In addition, the governance rules require disclosure of executive compensation and prohibit "golden parachutes"—lucrative benefits given to executives who are departing their jobs.

---

[56]The positions of manager and treasurer at smaller credit unions are considered equivalent of chief executive officer or chief financial officer.

NCUA's Total Loss Estimates Related to Credit Union Failures Were Unavailable

NCUA's audited financial statements for NCUSIF reported an allowance for loss of $777.6 million at December 31, 2010. This allowance for loss represents the difference between funds expended to close failed retail credit unions and the amounts NCUA estimates it will recover from the disposition of the failed retail credit unions' assets. Also, these financial statements reported additional estimated losses of about $1.23 billion as of December 31, 2010, associated with troubled credit unions considered likely to fail.

With respect to the Stabilization Fund, the 2010 audited financial statements were not yet final, as of December 19, 2011.[57] NCUA officials cited ongoing challenges in resolving and valuing failed corporate assets as contributing to the delays in finalizing the Stabilization Fund financial statements. We requested documentation adequate to support NCUA's estimates of losses from corporate failures, but NCUA was not able to provide the documentation we required. The NCUA OIG was provided with the same information that we obtained and told us that they were unable to verify NCUA's loss estimates. Absent this documentation, it is not possible to determine the full extent of losses resulting from corporate credit union failures. Moreover, without well-documented cost information, NCUA faces questions about its ability to effectively estimate the total costs of the failures and determine whether the credit unions will be able to pay for these losses.

Credit Unions Are Responsible for Repaying Loans, but Risks Remain

Credit unions are responsible for repaying NCUSIF and the Stabilization Fund, and NCUA has begun to assess credit unions for those losses. NCUA borrowed taxpayer funds from Treasury to fund NCUSIF and the Stabilization Fund to provide liquidity to the corporate system and it plans to repay the debt to Treasury with interest by 2021. Since 2009, NCUA has assessed credit unions a total of about $5 billion (about $1.7 billion for NCUSIF and $3.3 billion for the Stabilization Fund).

NCUA officials told us that they had analyzed the credit unions' ability to repay by determining the impact that varying assessment levels would have on the net worth ratios of both individual credit unions and the credit union system. NCUA considers factors such as the number of credit

---

[57]The NCUA 2010 Financial Statement Audit for Temporary Corporate Credit Union Stabilization Fund was released on December 27, 2011, after we completed our audit and therefore was not available for inclusion in this report.

unions that would fall below 2 percent capital or be subject to PCA's net worth restoration plan. In 2011, NCUA levied a $2 billion assessment for the Stabilization Fund. According to NCUA officials, NCUA determined that the credit union system had enough surplus capital to pay the assessment because of its strong return on assets of 0.86 percent for first three quarters of the year. NCUA determined that the assessment would result in around 811 credit unions having a negative return on assets. NCUA officials also noted that in a typical year about 10 to 20 percent of credit unions have had a negative return on assets. According to NCUA officials, the primary driver for the $2 billion Stabilization Fund assessment in 2011 was interest and principal on maturing medium-term notes that the corporates issued and that were to be repaid by the Stabilization Fund. NCUA officials told us that if they had found that the credit unions could not afford the Stabilization Fund assessment, they would have considered other options, such as issuing additional NCUA-guaranteed notes or unsecured debt.

Although NCUA officials have stated that the credit union system will bear the ultimate costs of corporate and credit union failures, risks to the taxpayers remain. However, many of the reforms are ongoing and NCUA continues to resolve the failure of U.S. Central and Wescorp, as will be discussed. Moreover, the ultimate effectiveness of NCUA's actions and associated costs remain unknown. As a result, whether the credit union system will be able to bear the full costs of the losses or how quickly NCUA will repay Treasury is unknown. Should the credit union system be unable to repay Treasury through NCUA assessments, taxpayers would have to absorb the losses.

NCUA Took Measures to Reduce Moral Hazard in Designing the Assistance and Reforms

Moral hazard occurs when a party insulated from risk may behave differently than it would behave if it were fully exposed to the risk. In the context of NCUA's actions to stabilize the credit union system, moral hazard occurs when market participants expect similar emergency actions in future crises, thereby weakening their incentives to manage risks properly. Furthermore, certain emergency assistance can also create the perception that some institutions are too big to fail. In general, mitigating moral hazard requires taking steps to ensure that any government assistance includes terms that make such assistance an undesirable last resort, except in the direst circumstances, and specifying when the government assistance will end. For example, we previously reported that during the 2007-2009 financial crisis, the federal government attached terms to the financial assistance it provided to financial institutions such as (1) limiting executive compensation,

(2) requiring dividends be paid to providers of assistance, and (3) acquiring an ownership interest—all of which were designed to mitigate moral hazard to the extent possible.[58]

NCUA designed actions to mitigate moral hazard at various stages of its effort to resolve and reform the corporate credit union system, but the effectiveness of these actions remains to be seen. Examples of the actions designed to mitigate moral hazard include terminating the corporates' management teams and eliminating their boards, issuing letters of understanding and agreement as a condition to entering the Share Guarantee Program, requiring a guarantee fee under the Liquidity Guarantee Program, requiring credit unions to repay the losses to NCUSIF and the Stabilization Fund, filing lawsuits against responsible parties, and requiring credit unions to disclose executive compensation. In addition, NCUA enhanced market discipline by requiring corporates to obtain capital from their member credit unions to remain in operation. That is, member credit unions decided whether to capitalize new corporates. As of October 30, 2011, the two of the four bridge corporates—Wescorp Bridge and U.S. Central Bridge—had either not succeeded in obtaining sufficient member capital (Wescorp) or had not attempted to do so because of a lack of anticipated demand (U.S. Central). They are both being wound down by NCUA.

---

[58]GAO, *Ongoing Challenges and Guiding Principles Related to Government Assistance For Private Sector Companies*, GAO-10-719 (Washington, D.C.: Aug. 3, 2010).

NCUA's Use of PCA and Other Enforcement Actions Illustrate the Need to Improve Their Effectiveness

Credit unions that triggered PCA had mixed results. Our analysis of credit unions that underwent PCA indicates corrective measures that were triggered earlier were generally associated with more favorable outcomes. We observed successful outcomes associated with PCA, but also noted inconsistencies in the presence and timeliness of PCA and other enforcement actions. Furthermore, in most cases, other discretionary enforcement actions to address deteriorating conditions either were not taken or taken only in the final days prior to failure. Other financial indicators could serve to provide an early warning of deteriorating conditions at credit unions.[59]

Use of PCA and Other Enforcement Actions Highlight the Need to Address Deteriorating Credit Unions Earlier

The number of credit unions in PCA significantly increased as the financial crisis unfolded (see fig. 5).[60] From January 1, 2006, through June 30, 2011, 560 credit unions triggered PCA. Specifically, of the 560 credit unions that entered PCA from January 1, 2006, through June 30, 2011, the vast majority (452) triggered PCA from January 2008 through June 2011.

---

[59]Regulators face a challenging trade-off between false positives (in this context, taking an action based on an incorrect prediction of credit union distress) and false negatives (in this context, failing to take an action based on an incorrect prediction of credit union health) in establishing a threshold or thresholds for capital or other indicators that might trigger intervention in a potentially troubled credit union. Striking the right balance between these two errors depends on the relative costs of each error, and other considerations.

[60]For our analyses, we refer to credit unions "in PCA" as those that were included in NCUA's PCA monitoring reports, requiring a proactive regulatory response. The PCA monitoring reports focus on those credit unions that NCUA classifies as undercapitalized, significantly undercapitalized, or critically undercapitalized. These credit unions are required to develop a net worth restoration plan when the credit union has a net worth ratio of less than 6 percent or has not met risked-based net worth requirements. Similarly, we refer to credit unions entering or "triggering PCA" as those that have been initially identified as undercapitalized, significantly undercapitalized, or critically undercapitalized (utilizing the original net worth ratio classification and date in the PCA monitoring reports) that require a proactive regulatory response. These reports do not include other credit unions that have earnings retention requirements under PCA (e.g., those with a net worth ratio between 6 and less than 7 percent).

Figure 5: Number of Credit Unions in PCA, January 2006 to June 2011

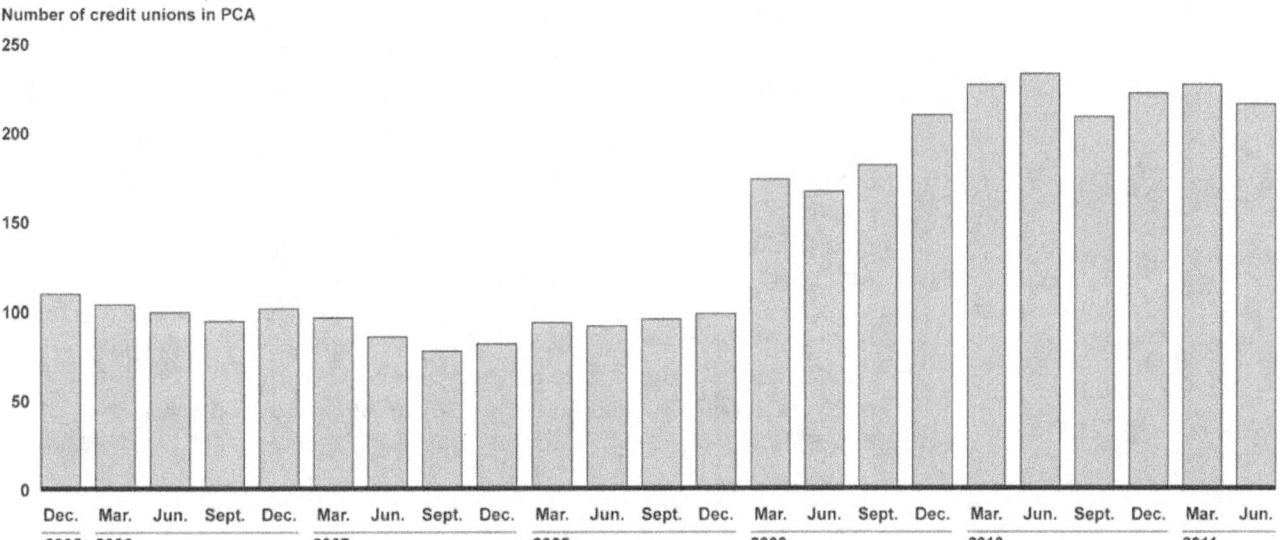

Number of credit unions in PCA

Source: GAO analysis of NCUA data.

Most credit unions that triggered PCA have not failed. Specifically, 69 of 85 credit unions that failed from January 2008 through June 2011 had previously triggered PCA. To examine these trends in more depth, we tracked a group of 275 credit unions that were subject to PCA from January 1, 2008, through June 30, 2009.[61] As of June 30, 2011, 40 percent of these 275 credit unions had merged with stronger credit unions, 39 percent remained in business, 19 percent failed, and 2 percent voluntarily liquidated. Of the credit unions still in business, 70 improved their net worth ratios in order to exit PCA; 37 remain in PCA.

From January 1, 2006, through June 30, 2011, most credit unions had capital at the undercapitalized level when PCA was triggered.[62] The timeliness of NCUA's application of PCA improved during the period. Specifically, for credit unions triggering PCA from January 2006 to December 2007, approximately 43 percent had initial capital levels that

---

[61]For the group of 275 credit unions, we observed outcomes of PCA for a minimum of 2 years subsequent to the date the credit union triggered PCA.

[62]Undercapitalized refers to a net worth ratio of less than 6 but at least 4 percent.

GAO-12-247 National Credit Union Administration

were significantly or critically undercapitalized. In contrast, for credit unions triggering PCA from January 2008 through June 2011, approximately 77 percent were classified as undercapitalized or greater, while less than a quarter (23 percent) entered at a significantly or critically undercapitalized level.

While our analysis revealed some favorable outcomes, we observed inconsistencies related to the presence and timeliness of PCA's implementation. For instance, PCA was not triggered for 16 of the 85 credit unions that failed from January 1, 2008, to June 30, 2011. The remaining 69 credit unions triggered PCA prior to failure, but did so at lower capital levels than the credit unions that triggered PCA as a whole during the same period (see fig. 6). Consequently, PCA had limited opportunity to address deteriorating conditions in credit unions that eventually failed, particularly when capital deteriorated quickly. In most cases, PCA was not initiated until less than 180 days prior to failure.

Figure 6: Capital Levels of All Credit Unions Triggering PCA versus Those That Failed, January 1, 2008, to June 30, 2011

Capital levels of credit unions entering PCA, January 2008 through June 2011

Capital levels of credit unions that entered PCA and subsequently failed from January 2008 through June 2011

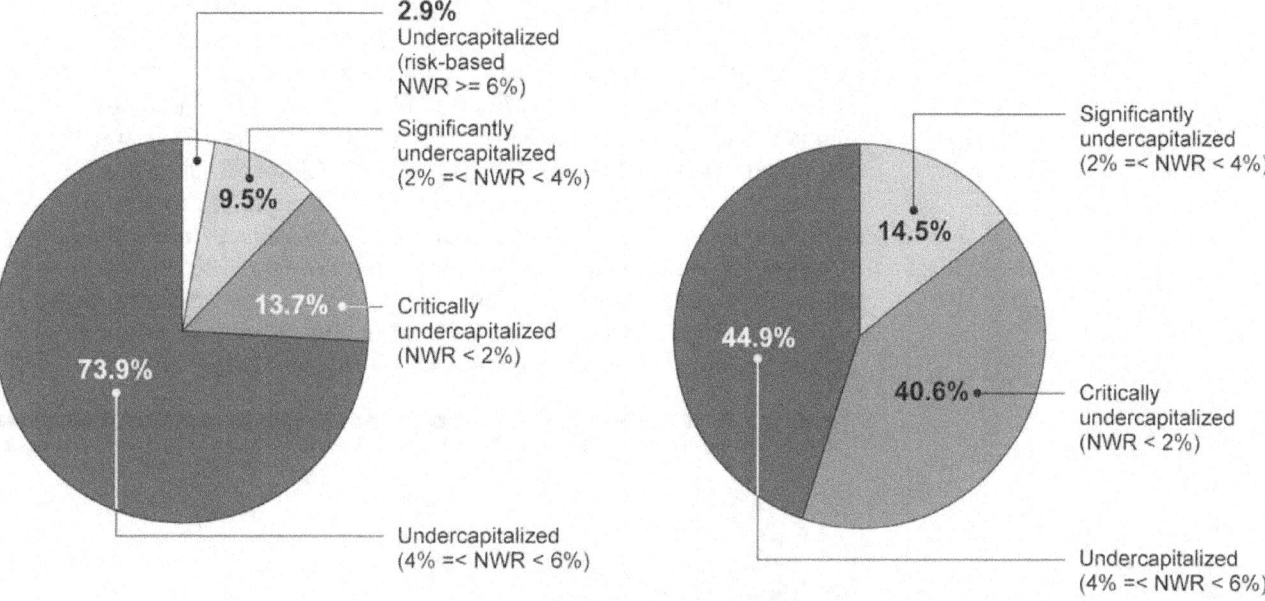

Source: GAO analysis of NCUA data.

Notes: Credit unions entering PCA also include newly chartered credit unions that are placed in PCA by regulators as a matter of practice. NWR means net worth ratio. The breakout of initial capital levels is shown for all 69 credit unions that entered PCA and subsequently failed from January 2008 through June 2011, including 7 credit unions that triggered PCA prior to 2008. A breakout of initial capital levels among 62 credit unions that triggered PCA from 2008 on was similar, with 45 percent triggering PCA at the undercapitalized level and 55 percent triggering PCA at the significantly or critically undercapitalized level.

Similar to the implementation of PCA measures, our analysis showed inconsistencies in the presence and timeliness of other discretionary enforcement actions for the credit unions that failed. The CAMEL composite ratings generally highlighted the deterioration of credit unions prior to failure. Specifically, our analysis showed:

- 50 of 85 failed credit unions received a CAMEL 3 composite rating prior to failure, with a median of 641 days prior to failure;

- 63 of 85 failed credit unions received a CAMEL 4 composite rating prior to failure, with a median of 365 days prior to failure; and

GAO-12-247 National Credit Union Administration

- 48 of 85 failed credit unions received a CAMEL 5 composite rating prior to failure, with a median of 96 days prior to failure.

Despite the deteriorating condition of these credit unions, in many cases, NCUA either did not take any non-PCA formal or informal enforcement action or took action only in the final days prior to failure (see fig. 7). For instance, for 42 of the 85 failed credit unions (49.4 percent) NCUA did not take any formal or informal enforcement action (non-PCA) on credit unions within 2 years prior to their failure. In some cases, when action was taken, it was not timely. For example, 12 of the 85 failed credit unions (14.1 percent) did not have an initial formal or informal non-PCA enforcement action until 180 days or less before failure. In the remaining 31 cases (36.5 percent), action was taken more than 180 days prior to the failure of the credit union. As discussed earlier, similar concerns about the presence and timeliness of enforcement actions were also frequently cited in MLRs and other reports issued by NCUA's OIG.

Figure 7: Timeliness of Other Non-PCA Enforcement Actions on Failed Credit Unions

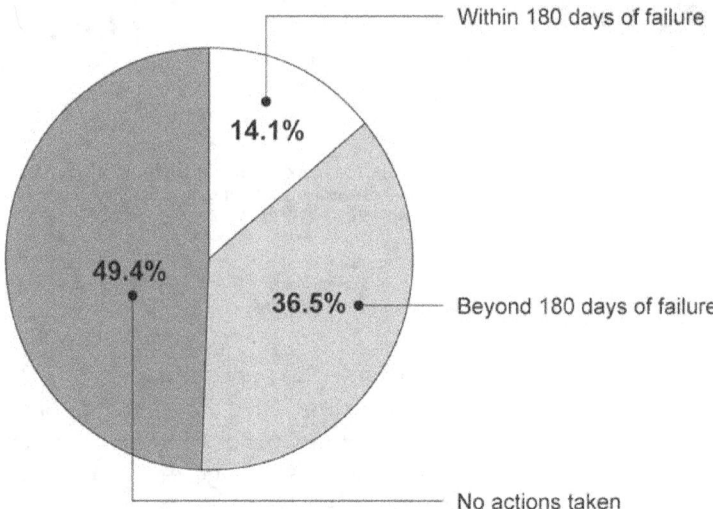

Source: GAO analysis of NCUA data.

Note: Figures are based on a 2 year look back period.

These results are also consistent with our recent work to assess the performance of PCA and other enforcement actions for banks.[63] In particular, we found that the presence and timeliness of enforcement actions (non-PCA) to address deteriorating banks were inconsistent. Furthermore, we noted that the effectiveness of PCA, as currently constructed, is limited because of its reliance on capital, which can lag behind other indicators of financial health. That is, problems with a bank's assets, earnings, or management typically manifest before these problems affect capital levels. Consequently, once an institution falls below PCA's capital standards, it may not be able to recover regardless of the regulatory action imposed.

Other Financial Indicators Could Help Identify Troubled Credit Unions Earlier than Capital

Multiple indicators of financial health highlight differences in asset quality, earnings, management, and liquidity between the failed and other credit unions well before failure, and may be helpful in detecting future distress. In considering other indicators for detecting early distress in credit unions, we reviewed data from regulatory filings from the fourth quarter of 2005 through the first quarter of 2011 for (1) the 85 credit unions that failed from January 2008 through June 2011 and (2) a group of 340 peer credit unions—the four closest credit unions in terms of total assets within the state as each failed credit union.[64] To compare the performance of these groups, we analyzed a range of indicators from the CAMEL rating that demonstrate asset quality, management, earnings, and liquidity. For assessing asset quality, we also looked at credit unions' risk exposure and credit performance.[65] Some indicators we analyzed showed differences between the failed credit unions and their peers, but were not necessarily strong indicators. Furthermore, using some of these indicators as early warning signs of distress could present different advantages and disadvantages—all of which would need to be considered.

---

[63]GAO-11-612.

[64]While a total of 340 peer credit unions reported their financial condition in regulatory filings during the entire period, the number of failed credit unions reporting declined over this period because credit unions stopped reporting after they failed. We also compared these groups against the industry—all credit unions that reported their financial condition in a regulatory filing for each quarter within the period.

[65]The indicators we chose for this review were based partially on the ability to obtain publicly available data across all credit unions.

Asset quality. We analyzed a number of indicators of asset quality. Specifically, we analyzed indirect loans as a percentage of total assets; payment-option, adjustable rate mortgages, and interest-only mortgage loans as a percentage of total assets; participation loans as a percentage of total assets; and MBLs as percentage of total assets. While these measures contribute to an understanding of the quality of assets credit unions may have in their portfolios, one measure we looked at—delinquency rates on MBLs—may be predictive of declining asset quality and deteriorating portfolio performance, and hence future failure. Delinquency rates on MBLs demonstrate that the credit performance of these loans for failed credit unions was significantly worse than the peers.

Figure 8: Delinquency Rates on MBLs for Failed Credit Unions Compared to the Peer Group, December 31, 2005, through March 31, 2011

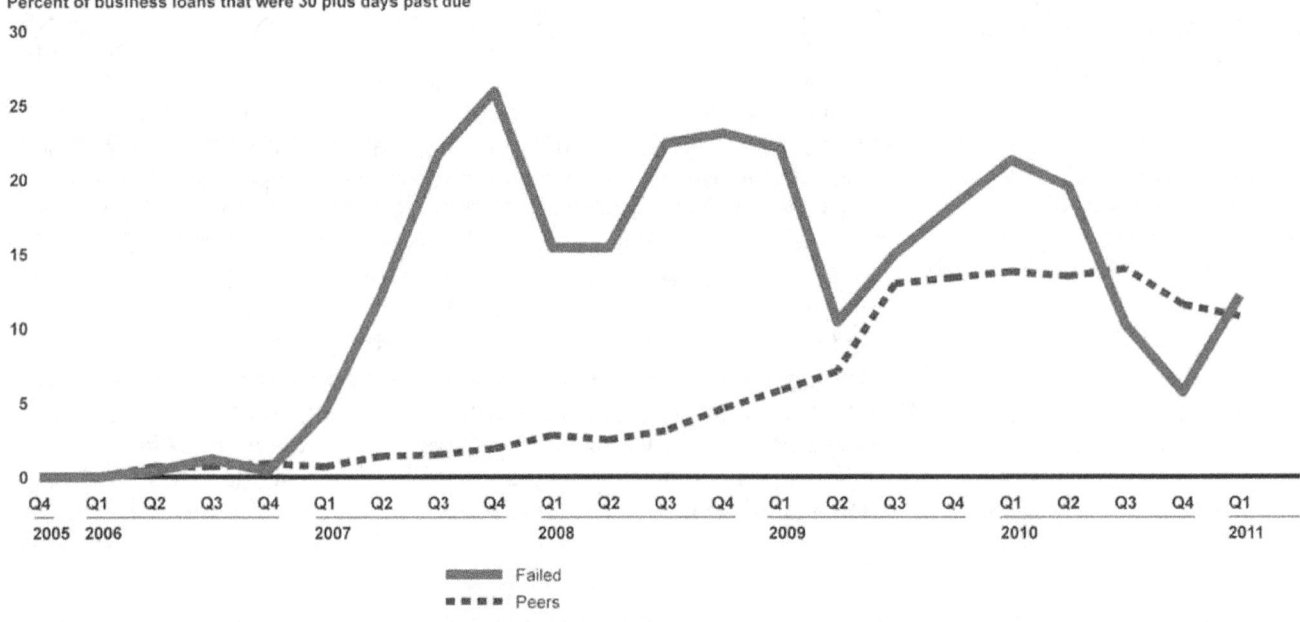

Percent of business loans that were 30 plus days past due

Source: GAO analysis of SNL Financial data.

Management. Operating expenses as a percentage of average total assets indicates how efficiently a credit union manages its business. Operating expenses can also be correlated with credit quality, as delinquent loans require more servicing. All other things equal, credit unions that have lower operating expense ratios are more profitable and able to retain more earnings than those with higher operating expense ratios. The failed credit unions had operating expenses nearly

GAO-12-247 National Credit Union Administration

1 percentage point higher than peer group at the fourth quarter of 2005, well before the financial crisis and the bulk of credit union failures. This difference continued to increase over time, peaking in the third quarter of 2008 but remained around 3 percentage points higher at the end of the period (see fig. 9).

Figure 9: Operating Expenses as a Percentage of Average Total Assets for Failed Credit Unions Compared to the Peer Group, December 31, 2005, through March 31, 2011

Percentage of average total assets operating expenses as a percentage of average total assets

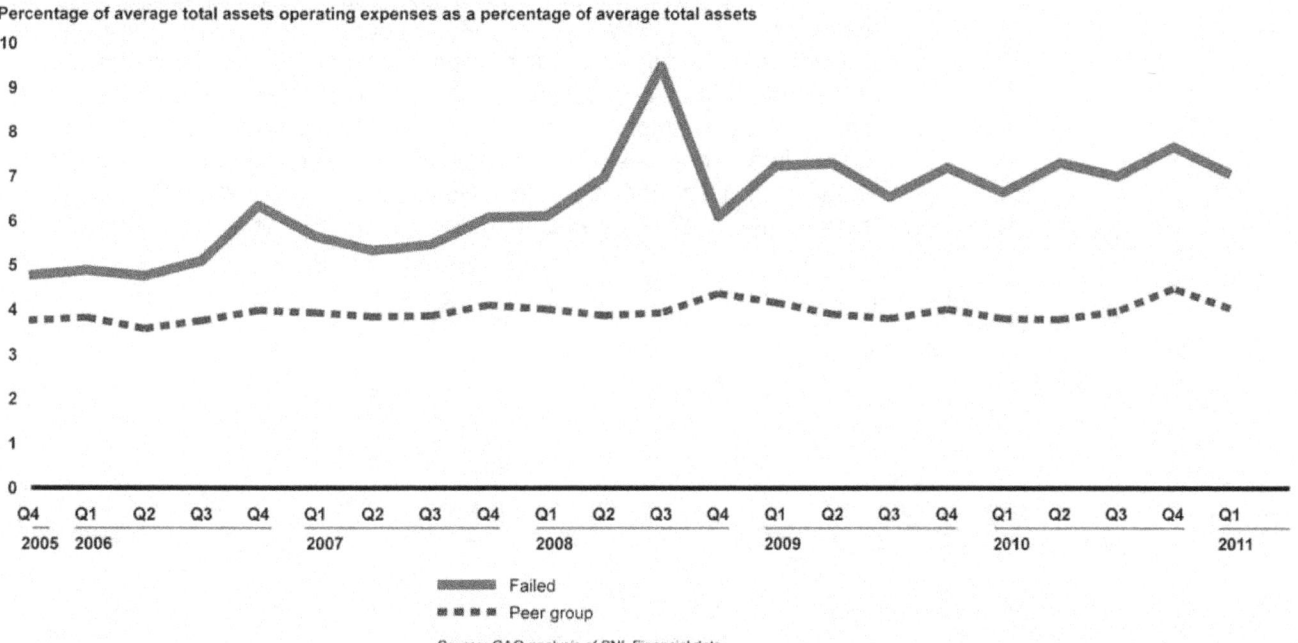

Failed

■ ■ ■ ■ Peer group

Source: GAO analysis of SNL Financial data.

Earnings. Net income as a percentage of assets indicates the profitability of institutions. Specifically, we examined two measures—costs of funds and return on assets—as indicators of earnings.[66] For most of the period of our analysis, the credit unions that eventually failed paid a higher

[66]The cost of funds measures the average interest rate that credit unions need to pay its creditors to fund its liabilities and indicates profitability.

average cost of funds compared with the peer group.[67] However, because the differences were slight, it did not appear to be a strong leading indicator and return on assets appeared to be a stronger leading indicator.

Return on assets is a commonly used measure of credit union financial performance and measures the net income or profit that a credit union generates as a percentage of its total assets.[68] Prior to the 2007-2009 financial crisis, the return on assets for the failed credit unions was similar to the peer group. However, as the financial crisis escalated through late 2007 and throughout 2008, the credit unions that eventually failed saw their performance deteriorate significantly, with the return on assets falling as low as negative 20 percent in the third quarter of 2008. During the same time period, the return on assets for the peer group had significantly smaller declines, and improved to levels near zero in 2008 through the first quarter of 2011 (see fig. 10).

---

[67] Specifically over the time period, the failed credit unions averaged a cost of funds of 1.66 percent, which was 19 basis points more than its peer group. The higher cost of funds impacted the failed credit unions' profitability and limited their accumulation of capital as compared to the peer group and industry. These percentage differences appeared small, but these differences may reflect differing levels of risk taking by individual credit unions.

[68] Quarterly numbers are annualized by multiplying the return by four.

Figure 10: Return on Assets for Failed Credit Unions Compared to the Peer Group, December 31, 2005, through March 31, 2011

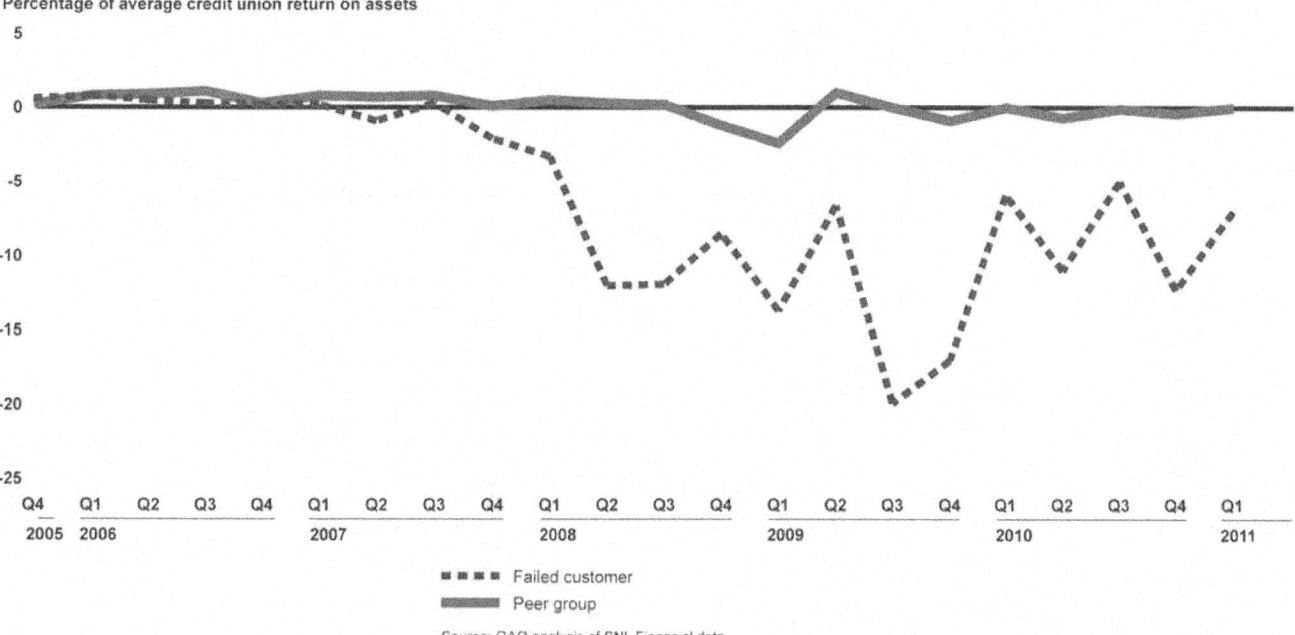

Percentage of average credit union return on assets

Source: GAO analysis of SNL Financial data.

Liquidity. Liquid assets as a percentage of total assets are a measure of credit unions' liquidity—that is, the ability to make payment on its short-term obligations.[69] This indicator showed that the failed credit unions consistently had fewer liquid assets compared to the peer group from December 31, 2005, through March 31, 2011. While the differences fluctuated throughout this time frame, the failed credit unions had at least 5 percentage points fewer liquid assets than the peer group, with the divergence growing to 14.3 percentage points compared to the peer group (see fig. 11).

[69]Liquidity is calculated as the sum of cash on hand, cash on deposit, cash equivalents, marketable securities, demand deposits and other assets that are readily convertible to cash.

Figure 11: Liquid Assets as a Percentage of Total Assets for Failed Credit Unions Compared to the Peer Group, December 31, 2005, through March 31, 2011

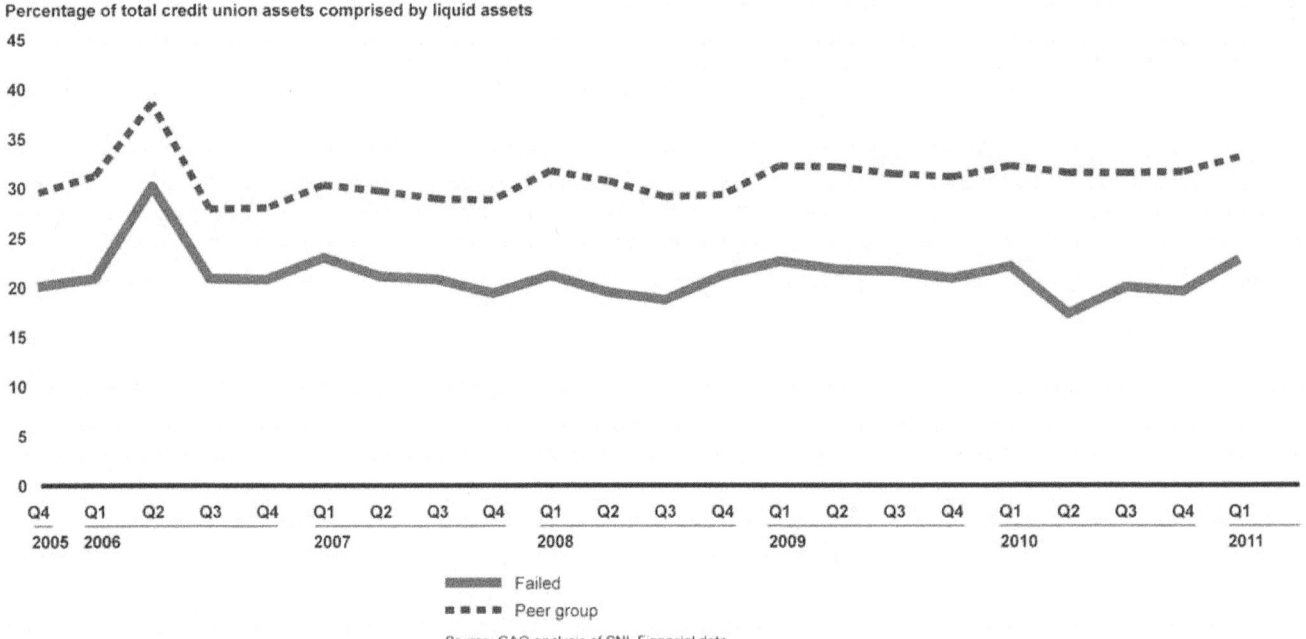

Percentage of total credit union assets comprised by liquid assets

Source: GAO analysis of SNL Financial data.

Conclusions

NCUA has taken steps to stabilize, resolve, and reform the corporate system. Many of the reforms are ongoing and NCUA continues to resolve the failures of U.S. Central and Wescorp. As a result, the ultimate effectiveness of NCUA's actions and associated costs remain unknown. Moreover, while the 2010 financial statements for NCUSIF are final—and record a loss—the 2010 financial statements for the Stabilization Fund were only recently released at the end of December 2011. Prior to the release of these statements, NCUA had estimated losses for the Stabilization Fund, but NCUA did not provide adequate documentation to allow us to verify the reasonableness and completeness of these estimates. Without well documented cost information, NCUA faces questions about its ability to effectively estimate the total costs of the failures and determine whether the credit unions will be able to pay for these losses.

Before the recent financial crisis, PCA was largely untested because the financial condition of the credit unions had been generally strong since PCA was enacted. With the failure of the 85 credit unions, the PCA

GAO-12-247 National Credit Union Administration

framework showed some weaknesses when addressing deteriorating credit unions. The main weakness of the PCA framework, as currently constructed in statute, stems primarily from tying mandatory corrective actions to only capital-based indicators. As previously reported, capital-based indicators have weaknesses, notably that they can lag behind other indicators of financial distress. Other alternative financial indicators exist or could be developed to help identify early warning signs of distress, which our analysis shows is a key to successful outcomes. Tying regulatory actions to additional financial indicators could mitigate these weaknesses and increase the consistency with which distressed credit unions would be treated. By considering which additional financial indicators would most reliably serve as an early warning sign of credit union distress—including any potential tradeoffs—and proposing the appropriate changes to Congress, NCUA could take the first steps in improving the effectiveness of PCA.

Recommendations for Executive Action

Given that the 2010 financial statements for the Stabilization Fund were not available for our review and NCUA was unable to provide us adequate documentation for their estimates as well as the identified shortcomings of current PCA framework, we recommend that NCUA take the following two actions.

1. To better ensure that NCUA determines accurate losses incurred from January 1, 2008, to June 30, 2011, we recommend that the Chairman of NCUA provide its OIG the necessary supporting documentation to enable the OIG to verify the total losses incurred as soon as practicable.

2. To improve the effectiveness of the PCA framework, we recommend that the Chairman of NCUA consider additional triggers that would require early and forceful regulatory actions, including the indicators identified in this report. In considering these actions, the Chairman should make recommendations to Congress on how to modify PCA for credit unions, and if appropriate, for corporates.

Agency Comments and Our Evaluation

We provided a draft of this report to NCUA and its OIG for their review and comment. NCUA provided written comments that are reprinted in appendix V and technical comments that we have incorporated as appropriate.

In its written comments, NCUA agreed with our two recommendations. Notably, NCUA stated that it had taken action to implement one of the recommendations by providing OIG with documentation of loss estimates for the Stabilization Fund as of December 31, 2010. It expects to provide additional documentation of loss estimates as of June 30, 2011, in January 2012. In its letter, NCUA also stated that the December 31, 2010, audited financial statements for the Stabilization Fund would be issued in the near future and described reasons for the delay in finalizing this audit. These reasons included the scope and magnitude of the corporate failures and the actions that NCUA had undertaken to resolve the corporate failures and strengthen its financial reporting systems. While NCUA acknowledged that some of the loss estimates were not finalized at the time of our audit, including the 2010 financial statements, it noted that the results from the valuation experts were complete and available. Our report recognizes the challenges that NCUA has faced in finalizing its financial statements and describes the actions that it has taken to stabilize, resolve, and reform the credit union system. However, as we reported, NCUA was unable to provide us with the documentation that we required to verify the reasonableness and completeness of the loss estimates for the Stabilization Fund. Subsequently, the *NCUA 2010 Financial Statement Audit for Temporary Corporate Credit Union Stabilization Fund* was released on December 27, 2011. Although NCUA has said that its analysis shows that the credit union system has the capacity to pay for the loss estimates, we continue to believe that without well-documented cost information, NCUA faces questions about its ability to effectively estimate the total costs of the failures and determine whether the credit unions will be able to pay for these losses. Taking the steps to address our recommendation will help NCUA address these questions.

In its written comments, NCUA also described its commitment to continued research and analysis to improve the effectiveness of PCA. In particular, NCUA cited its membership on the Federal Financial Institutions Examination Council and the Financial Stability Oversight Council. NCUA also noted that it was following developments related to the federal banking agencies' consideration of enhancements to PCA triggers, a step that we recommended in our report *Banking Regulation: Modified Prompt Corrective Action Framework Would Improve Effectiveness*.[70] NCUA agreed with the recommendation to consider other

---

[70]GAO-11-612.

triggers for PCA but noted that some of the potential financial indicators that we identified could have drawbacks. We also acknowledged in the report that multiple indicators of financial health could be used as early warning indicators and that the extent to which the financial indicators we identified could serve as strong early warning indicators might vary. Furthermore, using some of these indicators as early warning signs of distress could present different advantages and disadvantages—all of which would need to be considered. Nevertheless, we continue to believe that considering a range of potential indicators, including those identified in the report, is a necessary and important step in improving the effectiveness of PCA.

NCUA's letter also noted a potential "misconception" in the report and said that it recognized the need for timelier use of formal enforcement action, as evidenced in its response to OIG findings and recommendations. However, NCUA stated that nearly all failed credit unions received an enforceable regulatory action prior to failure, either through PCA or non-PCA authorities. In some cases, the failures occurred so abruptly that NCUA did not have a long lead time to take action. NCUA also stated that it had a strong record of employing PCA actions when credit unions tripped PCA triggers, as PCA actions are often more expedient forms of enforceable regulatory action. As discussed in the report, successful outcomes were associated with PCA in some cases. However, we also found inconsistencies in the presence and timeliness of PCA and other enforcement actions. Furthermore, we also found that other discretionary enforcement actions to address deteriorating conditions either were not taken or were taken only in the final days before the failure. Finally, the letter concluded that credit unions performed well during the recent financial crisis and that NCUA had successfully mitigated the failures that did occur. Our report describes the scope and magnitude of failures among corporates and credit unions and also notes that the 85 credit unions represented less than 1 percent of credit union assets as of 2008. Finally, we also described actions NCUA had taken to stabilize the credit union system, but we note that NCUA's examination and enforcement processes did not result in strong and timely actions to avert the failure of these institutions.

We are sending copies of this report to NCUA, the Treasury, and the Financial Stability Oversight Council, and other interested parties. The report is also available at no charge on the GAO website at http://www.gao.gov.

If you or your staffs have any questions about this report, please contact A. Nicole Clowers at (202) 512-8678 or clowersa@gao.gov. Contact points for our Office of Congressional Relations and Public Affairs may be found on the last page of this report. GAO staff that made major contributions to this report are listed in appendix V.

A. Nicole Clowers
Director
Financial Markets
and Community Investment

Appendix I: Status of OIG Recommendations to NCUA, as of October 30, 2011

During the period of November 2008 to October 2011, the National Credit Union Administration's (NCUA) Office of Inspector General (OIG) made 25 recommendations to NCUA to improve both corporate and credit union supervision, operations and financial reporting.[1] Six of the 25 recommendations were for corporates and 19 were for credit unions. NCUA has fully implemented 6 of the 25 recommendations relating to improving the corporate structure, corporate governance, examination processes, and call report data, as well as providing guidance on concentration risk. In addition, they have partially implemented another 10 recommendations—2 of these relate to corporate risk management and corporate examiner training. The other 8 partially implemented recommendations are related to improving the credit union examination process and financial monitoring of credit unions on areas such as fast growing and new business programs, third-party relationships, concentration risk, and ensuring credit union's take appropriate action to respond to documents of resolution (DOR).[2] Finally, NCUA has not yet implemented another 9 recommendations—6 of these recommendations are related to improving examination processes for credit unions with more than $100 million in assets, internal controls and documenting call report analysis. The remaining 3 recommendations that were not implemented relate to improving follow-up procedures for DORs. Furthermore, OIG officials have told us that 13 of the 19 partially or not implemented recommendations will likely be fulfilled with the issuance of the revised National Supervision Policy Manual (NSPM) in 2012. OIG

---

[1]These recommendations are from seven MLRs, *OIG Capping Report on Material Loss Reviews* (OIG-10-20) and *Review of NCUA's Document of Resolution Follow-up Process* (OIG-11-11). The seven MLRs include *Material Loss Review of Huron River Credit Union* (OIG-08-10), *Material Loss Review of U.S. Central Federal Credit Union* (OIG-10-17), *Material Loss Review of Western Corporate Federal Credit Union* (OIG-10-19), *Material Loss Review of Members United Corporate Federal Credit Union* (OIG-11-01), *Material Loss Review of Certified Federal Credit Union* (OIG-11-08), *Material Loss Review of Constitution Corporate Federal Credit Union* (OIG-11-09), and *Material Loss Review of Southwest Corporate Federal Credit Union* (OIG-11-10). It is OIG policy to follow-up with the agency on recommendations six months after they were issued. Four of these reports (OIG-11-08, OIG-11-09, OIG-11-10, and OIG-11-11) were issued within 6 months of October 30, 2011. Therefore, unless the agency had taken immediate action these recommendations would not be closed by the OIG at the time of this report.

[2]DORs are used by NCUA examiners to outline plans and agreements reached with credit union officials to reduce identified areas of unacceptable risk. DORs identify persons responsible and time frames for correction and may contain one or more action items. DOR action items include the corrective action credit union management needs to perform and address the examiner's concerns related to a specific risk area and risk factor.

GAO-12-247 National Credit Union Administration

officials have reviewed the draft revised NSPM and determined that it addresses their recommendations. Table 3 provides a summary of these recommendations and their status based on our evaluation of the information that NCUA and its OIG provided.

Table 3: NCUA's Implementation of OIG Recommendations, as of October 30, 2011

Issue	Recommendation	Status	Comments
Three-tier corporate structure	NCUA evaluate the current three-tier corporate structure and impose comprehensive changes to corporate regulations and guidance, as warranted, to strengthen individual corporates and the corporate system as a whole.	Implemented	On September 24, 2010, the NCUA Board issued a final rule establishing a new comprehensive framework for corporate safety and soundness. The OIG closed the recommendation based on this action.
Corporate guidance on concentration limits	Provide corporates with more definitive guidance on limiting investment portfolio concentrations by security type (i.e., agency-backed versus nonagency-backed securities); sector type (e.g., residential real estate versus nonresidential real estate); geography (e.g., less concentration in a single state); by supporting collateral (e.g., sub-prime; Alt-A; prime; adjustable rate mortgages with payment option, interest-only, and negative amortization features; etc.); and by issuer, originator, and servicer.	Implemented	On September 24, 2010, the NCUA board issued amendments to NCUA Rules and Regulations Part 704 that requires specific concentration limits by investment type and sector, including mortgage-backed securities (MBS). In addition, the final rule prohibits investments in private-label MBS and subordinated securities. The OIG closed the recommendation based on this action.
Corporate governance	Institute requirements for corporate board membership to eliminate conflicts of interest. Specifically, the NCUA should determine whether it is appropriate for retail corporate board members to sit on the boards of the top-tier corporate credit unions.	Implemented	The revised Corporate Rule requires a majority of a corporate board members be representatives of credit unions and limits a person serving on multiple corporate boards. The OIG closed the recommendation based on this action.
Corporate examiner training and guidance	Revise examiner guidance on evaluating aggressive growth strategies when such strategies appear to include increased credit risk for the corporate. Guidance should include the evaluation of growth strategies to determine their effect on the capital adequacy and overall safety and soundness of the corporate.	Implemented	According to NCUA officials, the new rule to eliminate the lower retained earnings reserve requirements of corporates will assist with managing growth as higher capital requirements have to be maintained. Consequently, the OIG closed the recommendation based on this action.

Issue	Recommendation	Status	Comments
	Provide NCUA examiners training to identify higher risk assets, especially if those assets are higher yielding products that involve a higher level of sophistication and several counterparties. Additionally, outside of previously raised recommendations for sector limit concentrations and diversification, NCUA should consider off-site monitoring enhancements of Call Report data to identify rapidly increasing holdings of certain types of assets and ensure that examiners and credit union management fully understand the risks posed by the products. NCUA should require credit unions to perform stress testing or scenario analysis to evaluate potential losses in the event of market dislocations or adjustments to other economic conditions.	Partially implemented	According to OIG officials, NCUA partially implemented this recommendation through the new corporate rules. However, the second part of this recommendation to enhance off-site monitoring and to require corporates to perform stress testing or scenario analysis has not yet been implemented.
Corporate risk management	Determine the best use of available resources to independently assess risk within corporates and other significant/complex institutions.	Partially implemented	According to the OIG, NCUA has indicated that there is an active working group identifying elevated risk posed by large, complex institutions and developing appropriate strategies to supervise those institutions. The OIG considers this an open recommendation.
Credit Union examination processes	NCUA management issue a Supervisory Letter to all federal and state examiners to alert them of the need to (1) analyze and understand financial ratios and trends individually and as a group and (2) thoroughly analyze pertinent qualitative data in order to adequately assess the safety and soundness of credit union operations.	Implemented	NCUA has issued guidance to credit unions and examiners on (1) the changing credit union business model, (2) mortgage and real estate market risks, and (3) risk focused supervision and monitoring. The OIG closed the recommendation based on this action.
	Expand examiner procedures to require examiners ensure amounts reported on the general ledger for all material accounts such as loans, member deposits, cash, and investments, reconcile to subsidiary ledgers and to the Call Report. Examiner procedures should also include reviewing bank and other key account reconciliations for unusual, large, or stale-dated reconciling items, as well as the underlying support.	Partially implemented	Effective January 1, 2011, NCUA required examiners to review and test bank reconciliations. However, the OIG suggests that NCUA should also require examiners to review and test other key balance sheet accounts and reconcile the balances to the credit union's call report. In addition, NCUA has revised the NSPM to require examiners that identify untimely or inaccurate bank reconcilements or other material out of balance accounts and require corrective action within 180 days. NCUA expects to implement the NSPM in 2012.
	Require examiners to document their consideration of external audit findings and recommendations in the Risk Assessment. Examiners should ensure examination procedures directly address the audit findings and examiners work papers adequately document the review.	Not implemented	NCUA has revised the draft NSPM to require examiners to assess transaction risk as high if significant or ongoing recordkeeping errors are identified. Additionally, the NSPM will require examiners to document review of the Supervisory Committee audit work papers and follow-up on material concerns. NCUA expects to implement the NSPM in 2012.

Issue	Recommendation	Status	Comments
Assigning Capital Adequacy, Asset Quality, Management, Earnings and Liquidity (CAMEL) ratings	Caution examiners that assigning CAMEL composite ratings of 1 or 2 to credit unions that implement new business strategies needs to be supported with compelling, verified mitigating factors. Such mitigating factors should consider things such as the institution's corporate governance, risk management controls, allowance for loan and lease losses methodologies, concentration limits, funding sources, underwriting standards, capital levels, and whether the mitigating factors are likely to be sustainable in the long-term.	Partially implemented	According to the OIG, NCUA has issued several letters to credit unions beginning in August 2008 on evaluating risk. According to NCUA officials, letters to credit unions are guidance for both credit unions and examiners. In addition, NCUA is in the process of revising the NSPM to address the evaluation of risk related to new business strategies. According to NCUA, it will implement the revised NSPM in 2012. The OIG considers this an open recommendation.
	Issue guidance regarding the evaluation of management with an emphasis on management integrity. The guidance should emphasize the various factors that should be considered when assessing the management component of the CAMEL rating system. The guidance should address the principles of the Risk Focused Exam program that need to differ when addressing management integrity issues versus issues of competence.	Not implemented	NCUA plans to evaluate this recommendation and if necessary issue additional guidance addressing how examinations should differ when addressing management integrity versus competency issues.
	Require a documented secondary review of the final CAMEL ratings by the Supervisory Examiner for all credit unions with more than $100 million in assets prior to issuance to credit union management.	Not implemented	According to the OIG, NCUA is in the process of revising the NSPM to require senior examiner reviews of any credit union with assets exceeding $250 million. NCUA expects to implement the revised NSPM in 2012. The OIG considers this an open recommendation.
Monitoring credit union call reports	Issue a national instruction placing more emphasis on quarterly monitoring of Call Reports including developing offsite monitoring triggers and specific procedures to more easily "red flag" areas to be investigated as well as provide a specific time allocation.	Partially implemented	NCUA is in the process of revising the NSPM to require that examiners document their quarterly review of call reports, financial performance and national risk reports. NCUA expects to implement the NSPM in 2012. In addition, NCUA has taken steps to enhance quarterly regional risk reports, issued guidance on the identification and mitigation of risk, provided instruction to examiners, and revised the minimum examination scope. The OIG considers this an open recommendation.

Issue	Recommendation	Status	Comments
	Require examiners to document and retain the specific procedures and analysis performed during their quarterly review of the 5300 Call Reports. This analysis should then be forwarded to the Supervisory Examiner for review.	Not implemented	According to NCUA, it has responded to this recommendation by enhancing quarterly regional risk reports to detect excessive growth of various loan and investment products. In addition, NCUA is in the process of revising the NSPM to require examiners to document the quarterly Call Report and Financial Performance Report reviews and developing an automated system for examiners, senior examiners, and regional office staff to document and review quarterly risk trends. The OIG considers this an open recommendation.
Credit union concentration risk	Require a breakout of unfunded commitments by loan type on the 5300 Call Report to facilitate analysis and to better track loan concentrations.	Implemented	NCUA has added data fields to the credit union Call Report to capture more detail regarding unfunded commitments by loan type. The OIG closed the recommendation based on this action.
	Determine whether to propose or change regulatory guidance to establish limits or other controls for concentrations that pose an unacceptable safety and soundness risk and determine an appropriate range of examiner response to high-risk concentrations.	Partially implemented	NCUA has taken steps to implement this recommendation, including providing instruction on risk identification and problem resolution and issuing guidance on addressing concentration risk. In addition, NCUA is in the process of revising the prompt corrective action (PCA) regulations so that the calculation of minimum net worth level will place additional emphasis on credit concentrations on a credit union balance sheet. According to the OIG, the recommendation will be closed after NCUA revises this regulation.
	Develop a more specific process, such as trigger reports or standards, so examiners can better identify, analyze, and monitor loan concentrations during exams, as well as between exams.	Partially implemented	NCUA has taken steps to implement this recommendation, including enhanced quarterly regional risk reports to identify excessive growth in loan and investment products, updated national risk reports to identify concentration risk, and issued guidance to credit unions and examiners on concentration risk. In addition, NCUA is in the process of updating examination software to provide triggers to guide examiner's review of concentration risk. The OIG considers this an open recommendation.

Issue	Recommendation	Status	Comments
New program or service and third-party due diligence at credit unions	Re-emphasize examination guidance for third-party relationships, with particular attention to the assessment of the risk the relationship may pose to the credit union's safety and soundness.	Partially implemented	NCUA has taken steps to implement this recommendation, including issuing guidance to credit unions and examiners and instruction to examiners on assessing the third-party relationships. In addition, NCUA has updated credit union service organizations (CUSO) regulations and required that all credit union examinations review third-party vendor relationships. NCUA is in the process of pursuing the enforcement authority over CUSOs, enhance supervision and examination of CUSOs, and improve the reporting of CUSO data to NCUA. The OIG considers this an open recommendation.
	Develop examination guidance for due diligence over new or fast growing programs and areas of emphasis, with particular attention to the risk the new program or new area may pose to the credit union's safety and soundness.	Partially implemented	According to the OIG, NCUA has taken steps to implement this recommendation, including issuing guidance to credit unions and examiners, instruction to examiners on identifying risk on new business lines and third-party due diligence. In addition, NCUA has updated the national risk reports to identify growth trends and new products or services, developed regional programs for onsite exams at high-risk credit unions, and required that all credit union examinations review third-party vendor relationships. However, NCUA is in the process of revising the NSPM to address the evaluation of risk related to new business strategies and expects to implement it in 2012. The OIG considers this an open recommendation.
Credit union examination quality control	Review the current requirements and levels that trigger a Quality Control Review and expand the process as necessary. Provide national guidelines for the Quality Control Review process so that all regions are consistent in their reviews.	Not implemented	According to the OIG, NCUA is in the process of revising the requirements that trigger an examination quality control review. This revision also required that senior examiners document their review of all examination reports. These revisions will be in the NSPM, which NCUA expects to implement in 2012. The OIG considers this an open recommendation.
	Require Supervisory Examiners to provide a written response to the results of Quality Control Review on any recommendations made by the Quality Control Review	Not implemented	According to the OIG, NCUA is in the process of revising the NSPM to require Supervisory Examiners to provide a written response when material issues are noted for an exam report. NCUA expects to implement the NSPM in 2012. The OIG considers this an open recommendation.

Issue	Recommendation	Status	Comments
Document of resolution follow-up process	Determine whether credit unions with repeat DORs have taken appropriate corrective action. In the event that corrective action has not been taken, examiners should be instructed to elevate the supervisory response, including the taking of enforcement action when necessary.	Partially implemented	According to the OIG, NCUA has issued guidance to credit unions and examiners and provided instruction on the administrative remedies available and timely resolution of problems. In addition, NCUA has enhanced on-site supervision requirements for troubled credit unions in one region. NCUA is in the process of revising the NSPM, which it expects to implement in 2012, to require the review of repeat DORs and other unresolved issues as part of the exam quality control review process. The OIG considers this an open recommendation.
	Develop a standardized DOR monitoring process requiring the Office of Examination and Insurance and the regional offices to generate and analyze DOR database reports on a regularly defined basis including, but not limited to the DOR Aging Months of Unresolved Report.	Not implemented	According to NCUA, the Office of Examinations and Insurance and Office of the Chief Information Officer will work together to improve the DOR reports thereby strengthening the regions ongoing monitoring and reporting of DOR items. In addition, additional guidance will be incorporated into the NSPM to be implemented in 2012 and training on the proper use of the DOR during NCUA's 2012 National Conference. The OIG considers this an open recommendation.
	Require written responses from credit union management, regardless of the composite CAMEL rating, for all DOR items not resolved within the established timeframes.	Not implemented	According to the OIG, NCUA has revised the draft NSPM and plans to require written responses for all DORs within a prescribed timeframe, regardless of the credit union's composite CAMEL rating. NCUA expects to implement the NSPM in 2012. The OIG considers this an open recommendation.
	Ensure regional staff takes stronger supervisory actions when a credit union fails to correct DOR items.	Not implemented	According to the OIG, NCUA has revised the draft NSPM to require more stringent administrative actions when credit unions do not resolve DORs in the agreed time frame. NCUA expects to implement the NSPM in 2012. The OIG considers this an open recommendation.

Source: GAO analysis of NCUA and OIG data.

Appendix II: Objectives, Scope, and Methodology

Legislation enacted in January 2011 requires us to examine NCUA's supervision of the credit union system and the use of PCA. This report examines (1) what is known about the causes of failures among corporates and credit unions since 2008; (2) the steps that NCUA has taken to resolve these failures and the extent to which its actions were designed to protect taxpayers, avoid moral hazard, and minimize the cost of corporate resolutions; and (3) NCUA's use of PCA and other enforcement actions. In addition, we reviewed NCUA's implementation of its OIG recommendations. (See app. I.)

Analysis of Causes of Failures among Corporates and Credit Unions

To identify the causes of failures among corporates and credit unions, we obtained and analyzed NCUA documents, including Material Loss Reviews (MLR), postmortem reports, Board Action Memorandums (BAM), and other relevant documents. To corroborate this information, we also assessed the asset size and investment concentrations for all failed and nonfailed corporates by conducting analyses of data from SNL Financial—a financial institution database—on corporates' investment portfolios from January 2003 to September 2010.[1] We obtained and analyzed NCUA data related to conservatorships and resolution actions taken from January 2008 to June 2011 to determine the number and causes of corporates' and credit union failures. We further assessed credit union member business loan participation as a percentage of total loans for both failed and their peer credit unions that did not fail from December 2005 to January 2011. To identify credit union failures related to fraud, we reviewed data, analyzed reports and documents by NCUA and its OIG on each of the failed credit unions from January 2008 to June 2011. To determine loss data from the corporates' and credit union failures, we reviewed NCUA's 2008, 2009, and 2010 annual reports; MLRs; BAMs; and NCUA data on losses to National Credit Union Share Insurance Fund (NCUSIF) and the Temporary Corporate Credit Union Stabilization Fund (Stabilization Fund). We interviewed NCUA's OIG, Office of Corporate Credit Unions, Office of Capital Markets, Chief Financial Officer, and Office of Examination and Insurance to obtain their perspectives on the causes of the corporates' and credit union failures. We further met with credit union industry associations to obtain their views on NCUA's efforts to reform the corporate credit union system. We

---

[1]We used SNL Financial to analyze the levels of private-label MBS held by corporates. This included both private-label MBS and secondary mortgage and home equity loan asset-backed securities.

assessed the reliability of the SNL and NCUA data used for this analysis
and determined that these data were sufficiently reliable for our purposes.

Analysis of Actions Taken by NCUA to Stabilize the Credit Union System

To assess the steps that NCUA has taken to stabilize, resolve, and
reform the corporate and credit union system, we reviewed NCUA
documents and data including BAMs; MLRs; NCUA annual reports from
2008, 2009, and 2010; audited financial statements; NCUA's Corporate
Stabilization and Resolution Plan; and NCUA-commissioned reports; in
addition to testimonies at relevant congressional hearings and planning
documents.[2] To determine actions taken to reform the corporate system,
we reviewed NCUA's proposed and final rules and interviewed NCUA's
General Counsel to discuss the potential impact of these rules and their
effective dates. To determine NCUA's assessments for credit unions' and
their ability to repay, we reviewed BAMs, NCUA's scenario analyses for
its credit union assessments and loss estimates, and interviewed NCUA
officials. We requested detailed information on NCUA's loss estimates for
NCUSIF and Stabilization Fund; NCUA provided some information but it
was not sufficient for us to determine the reasonableness and
completeness of these estimates. To determine the steps that NCUA took
to reduce moral hazard, we compared the actions taken to stabilize,
resolve and reform the credit union system to principles cited in our past
work on providing federal financial assistance.[3]

Analysis of PCA Outcomes, Ratings Downgrades, Enforcement Actions and Other Indicators

To assess the outcomes of PCA, we reviewed the outcomes of credit
unions as a whole that were subject to PCA from January 1, 2006,
through June 30, 2011. Additionally, we tracked a group of credit unions
that were subject to PCA from January 1, 2008, through June 30, 2009,
during the 2007-2009 financial crisis to identify those credit unions that (1)
failed, (2) survived and remained in PCA, and (3) survived and exited
PCA. To determine the actions that NCUA took to address deteriorating

---

[2]NCUA commissioned a number of reports to assist them in estimating losses and
determining options for addressing the failures of the corporates, including reports by
Kamakura Corporation, PIMCO, and Barclay's Capital. In addition, while we reviewed
NCUA's 2010 annual report, losses for the Stabilization Fund were not included, the
NCUA 2010 Financial Statement Audit for Temporary Corporate Credit Union Stabilization
Fund was not released until December 27, 2011, after we had completed our audit.

[3]GAO-10-719.

credit unions, we reviewed regulatory information that included CAMEL
ratings, enforcement action data, and PCA-related activities over a 2 year
period prior to each credit union failure from January 1, 2008, through
June 30, 2011. Specifically, we analyzed the instances and dates of
CAMEL downgrades, enforcement actions taken, and PCA-related
actions to determine whether and when actions were taken.[4]

To assess the utility of various financial indicators in detecting credit unions'
distress, we reviewed the OIG's MLRs, NCUA's postmortem studies, and
our previous work on PCA.[5] We compared failed credit unions to peer
credit unions that did not fail to assess their performance on numerous
financial indicators, such as return on assets, operating expenses and
liquid assets as an early warning of financial distress. We also compared
the failed credit unions and their peers to credit union industry averages
across the same period. In considering other indicators for detecting early
distress in credit unions, we reviewed data from regulatory filings from the
fourth quarter of 2005 through the first quarter of 2011 for three groups: (1)
the 85 credit unions that failed from January 2008 to June 2011; (2) a
group of 340 peer credit unions—the four closest credit unions in terms of
total assets within the state as each failed credit union; and (3) all credit
unions that reported their financial condition in a regulatory filing for each
quarter within the period.[6] To compare the performance of these three
groups, we chose a range of indicators from the CAMEL rating that
demonstrates asset quality (A), management (M), earnings (E), and
liquidity (L). For assessing asset quality, we also looked at credit unions'
risk exposure and credit performance.[7] To perform this work, we relied on
data from SNL Financial.

---

[4]NCUA rates credit unions using the CAMEL system, which stands for capital adequacy,
asset quality, management, earnings, and liquidity. The ratings are on a scale of 1 to 5,
with 1 being the best and 5 the worst.

[5]GAO-11-612.

[6]While a total of 340 peer credit unions reported their financial condition in regulatory
filings during the entire period, the number of failed credit unions reporting declined over
this period because credit unions stopped reporting after they failed.

[7]The indicators we chose for this review were based partially on the ability to obtain
publicly available data across all credit unions. Regulators could request other information
that would be useful for selecting additional financial indicators, such as the charge-off
data for certain asset classes.

We assessed the reliability of the SNL Financial database and NCUA's enforcement data used in our analyses, and found these data to be sufficiently reliable for our purposes.

Analysis of NCUA's Actions to Address OIG Recommendations

To determine the status of NCUA's implementation of OIG recommendations, we reviewed the OIG's corporate and credit union MLRs and their recommendation tracking documents and interviewed NCUA and NCUA's OIG officials.

We conducted this performance audit from May 2011 to December 2011 in accordance with generally accepted government auditing standards. Those standards require that we plan and perform the audit to obtain sufficient, appropriate evidence to provide a reasonable basis for our findings and conclusions based on our audit objectives. We believe that the evidence obtained provides a reasonable basis for our findings and conclusions based on our audit objectives.

Appendix III: NCUA Temporary Stabilization and Guarantee Programs

To help stabilize the credit union system, NCUA created four new programs to provide liquidity to corporates. NCUA initiated two of these new programs, the Credit Union System Investment Program (CU-SIP) and the Credit Union Homeowners' Affordability Relief Program (CU-HARP) in early 2009. Due to the restriction preventing the Central Liquidity Facility (CLF) from lending directly to the corporate credit unions, NCUA designed both programs, CU-SIP and CU-HARP, so that the CLF would lend to the credit unions, which agreed that they in turn would invest in NCUA-guaranteed notes issued by corporates. Starting in January 2009, corporates were required to use the invested funds to pay down their external secured debt. Money from the corporates' debt issuances were used to free up collateral and to pay back loans made by the credit unions. In exchange for participating in the programs, the corporates were required to pay CLF borrowing costs to credit unions and an additional fee to the credit unions as an incentive for them to participate in the programs. CLF lending to credit unions totaled approximately $8.2 billion under CU-SIP and about $164 million under CU-HARP. All borrowings for both programs were repaid in 2010.

- *CU-SIP.* Credit unions received a 25-basis-point spread over the cost of borrowing from the CLF for investing in 1-year CU-SIP note issued by participating corporate credit unions. Lending from the CLF for the CU-SIP started in January 2009 and ended in March 2009, totaling approximately $8.2 billion. All borrowings were repaid by the credit unions to the CLF by the respective months in 2010 (see fig. 12).

Figure 12: Overview of CU-SIP

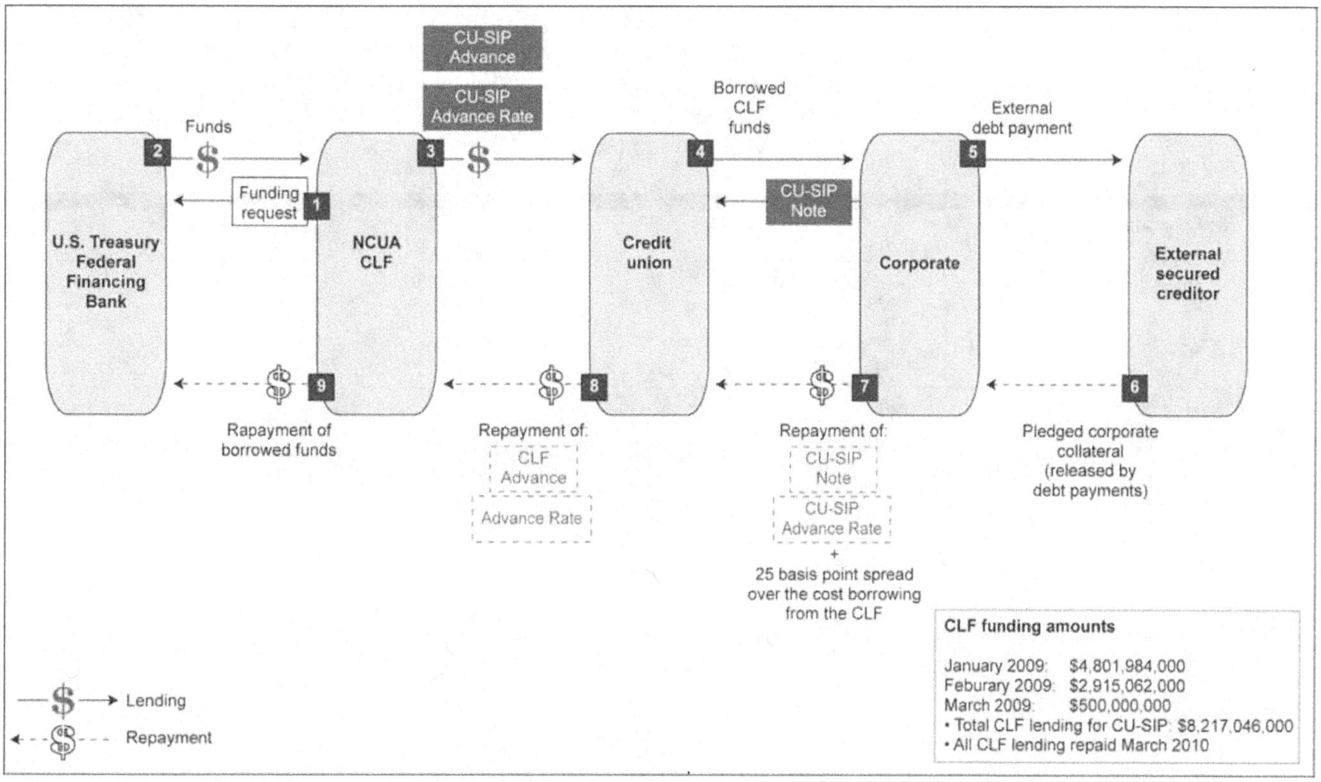

CU-SIP
Advance

CU-SIP
Advance Rate

Borrowed
CLF
funds

External
debt payment

Funds

Funding
request 1

CU-SIP
Note

U.S. Treasury
Federal
Financing
Bank

NCUA
CLF

Credit
union

Corporate

External
secured
creditor

Rapayment of
borrowed funds

Repayment of:

CLF
Advance

Advance Rate

Repayment of:

CU-SIP
Note

CU-SIP
Advance Rate

+

25 basis point spread
over the cost borrowing
from the CLF

Pledged corporate
collateral
(released by
debt payments)

CLF funding amounts

January 2009: $4,801,984,000
Feburary 2009: $2,915,062,000
March 2009: $500,000,000
• Total CLF lending for CU-SIP: $8,217,046,000
• All CLF lending repaid March 2010

$ → Lending

$ - - - Repayment

Source: GAO analysis of NCUA data.

- *CU-HARP.* This 2-year program was designed to assist struggling homeowners by temporarily facilitating modifications to their monthly mortgage payments.[1] Credit unions invested in CU-HARP Notes from participating corporates. These notes had 1-year maturities and the option to extend the date of maturity for an additional year. The extension of the program's 1-year maturity depended on the credit union's continued good standing and available CLF funding. The CLF lent approximately $164 million to credit unions under the CU-HARP.

---

[1]A 1-year program with an optional 1-year extension, subject to the credit worthiness of participating credit unions. This program is similar to the Department of the Treasury's Home Affordable Modification Program, which provided assistance to homeowners through a cost-sharing arrangement with mortgage holders and investors to reduce monthly mortgage payment amounts of those at risk of foreclosure to affordable levels.

GAO-12-247 National Credit Union Administration

All remaining notes under the program matured in December 2010 and the credit unions repaid all borrowings. The corporates paid a bonus to the credit unions, which was tied to a 50 percent reduction relief in mortgage payments to homeowners. According to NCUA, CU-HARP was not very successful as the program's design for credit unions to earn the bonus was complex and the time frame in which to apply was limited (see fig. 13).

Figure 13: Overview of CU-HARP

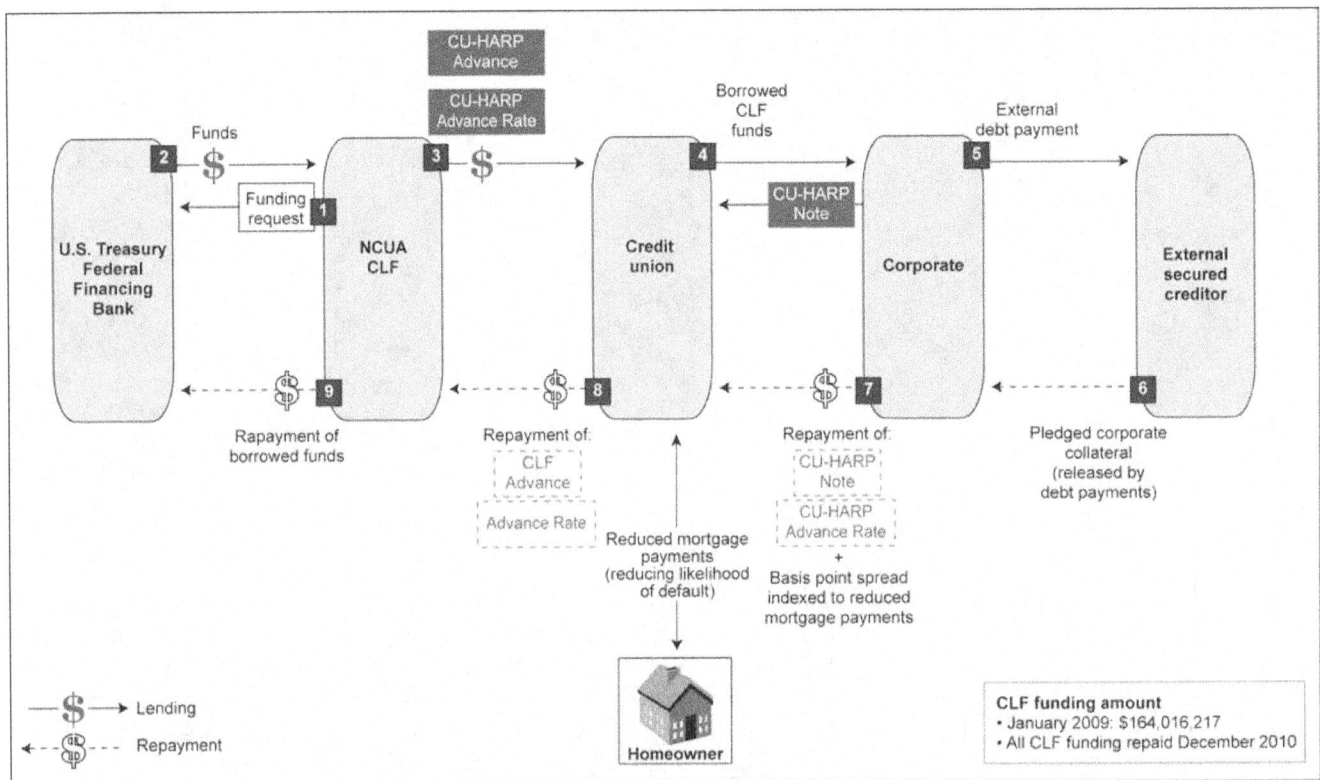

Source: GAO analysis of NCUA data.

NCUA created two temporary guarantee programs in late 2008 and early 2009 called the Temporary Corporate Credit Union Liquidity Guarantee Program (Liquidity Guarantee Program) and Temporary Corporate Credit Union Share Guarantee Program (Share Guarantee Program) to help stabilize confidence and dissuade withdrawals by credit unions, in an attempt to avoid a run on the corporates by member credit unions. These programs provided temporary guarantees on unsecured offerings by corporates and shares of credit unions held by corporates in excess of $250,000.[2] NCUA originally included all corporates under both guarantee programs for a limited time after signing a letter of understanding and agreement limiting activities and compensation. It later extended the programs to corporates chose not to opt out of the programs.

- *Liquidity Guarantee Program.* NCUA guaranteed the timely payment of principal and interest of all corporates' unsecured debt.[3] The program's debt issuance deadline was September 2011, with debt maturing no later than June 2017. However, the program was later revised so that any unsecured debt issued after June 2010 would mature no later than September 2012. NCUA stated that this revision was necessary to focus on short-term liquidity needs and bring the program's deadline in line with its other stabilization efforts (see fig. 14).

[2]Unsecured debt is debt that is not collateralized. That is it has no supporting collateral or other guarantee securing the debt offering.

[3]This program is similar to the Federal Deposit Insurance Corporation's Temporary Liquidity Guarantee Program, which temporarily guaranteed newly-issued senior unsecured debt of insured depository institutions and most U.S. holding companies.

Figure 14: Timeline for the Liquidity Guarantee Program

NCUA extended program coverage to all corporates issuing unsecured debt.

Debt issued:

Corporates were given the option to extend their coverage in the program. If electing to participate, unsecured debt issuances may be issued up to June 30, 2010, and maturing no later than June 30, 2017.

NCUA revised the program such that unsecured debt issued after June 30, 2010, must mature on or before September 30, 2012. Debt issued after June 30, 2010, with a maturity later than September 30, 2012, is not covered under the program.

Guarantee:

Certain unsecured debt issuances guaranteed by NCUSIF.

Unsecured debt issuances guaranteed by the Stabilization Fund on June 2009 and after.

J F M A M J J A S O N | J F M A M J J A S O N | J F M A M J J A S O N | J F M A M J J A S O N | J F M A M J J A S | J F M A M J

2009   2010   2011   2012   2017

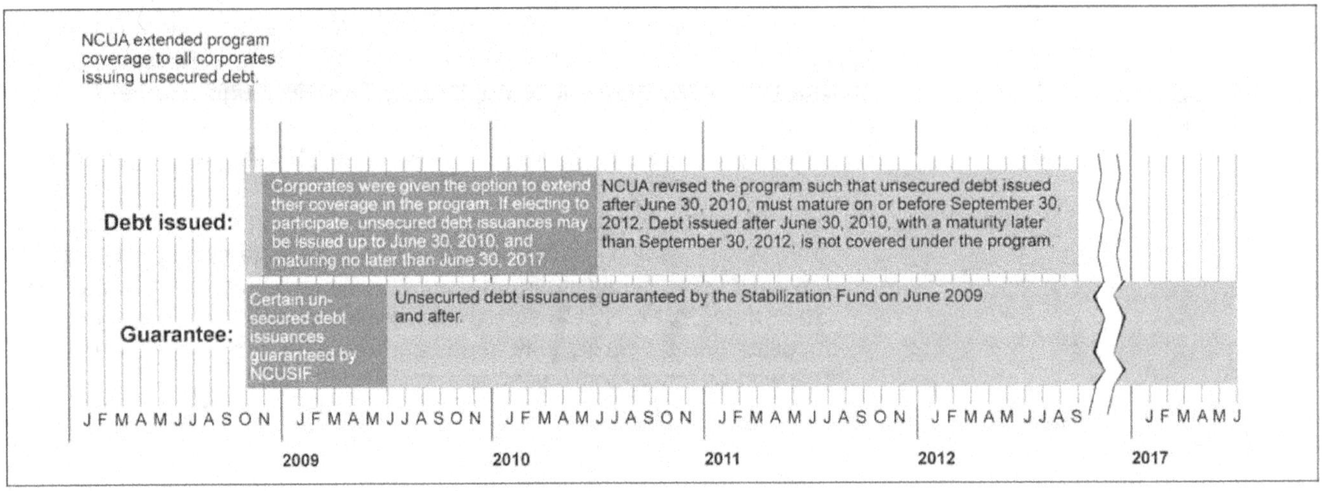

Source: GAO analysis of NCUA data.

- *Share Guarantee Program.* This program largely mirrors the Liquidity Guarantee Program. That is, NCUA guaranteed credit union shares in excess of $250,000 through February 2009, with the option of continuing participation in the program through December 2010. NCUA revised the program in May 2009 to extend the program's deadline to December 2012 and shortened the length of the program's coverage to shares with maturities of 2 years or less (see fig. 15).

Figure 15: Timeline for the Share Guarantee Program

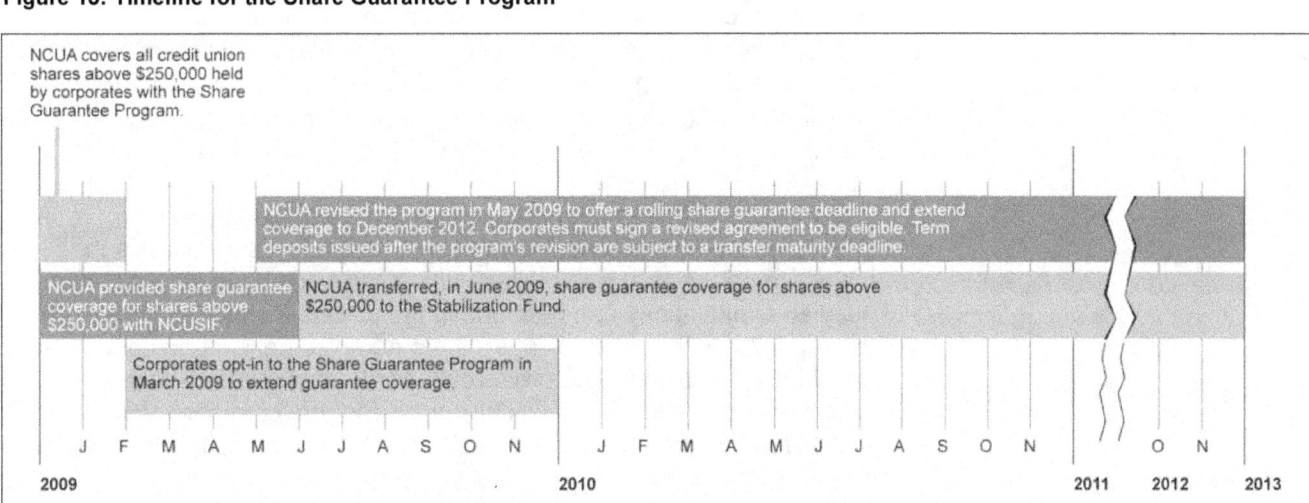

Source: GAO analysis of NCUA data.

In mid-2009, NCUA transferred obligations from both the Liquidity Guarantee and Share Guarantee programs to the Stabilization Fund to limit NCUSIF's losses stemming from any future corporate losses.[4] According to NCUA officials, NCUSIF was obligated to provide for any guarantee payments that might arise from either the Liquidity Guarantee Program or the Share Guarantee Program. Based on NCUA's 2009 financial statements, no guarantee payments were required for either program; however, as of December 19, 2011, audited 2010 financial statements for the Stabilization Fund were not available.

---

[4]The Liquidity Guarantee Program and the Share Guarantee Program provided guarantee coverage in the event that a corporate participating in either program would not be able to fulfill any of its payment obligations. This guarantee coverage has been transferred from NCUSIF to the Stabilization Fund.

Appendix IV: Summary of NCUA's 2010 Corporate Rule

On September 24, 2010, the NCUA Board adopted comprehensive new rules to govern corporates.[1] Following its initial publication the final rule, the corporate rules underwent several technical corrections and five additions to the corporate rule were published on April 29, 2011.[2] The corporate rule affect several parts of title 12 of the Code of Federal Regulations but is codified primarily in 12 C.F.R. Part 704.

This table provides an overview of the corporate rule as initially published in October 2010 and later amended in April 2011. It summarizes the major provisions at a general level and gives references to where more detailed explanations can be found in the preambles of the October 2010 and April 2011 final rulemakings. The preambles describe in considerable detail the rationales for the provisions, section-by-section analyses of each provision, what NCUA initially proposed, the comments it received and its response to them, and how the final provisions differ from those originally proposed.

---

[1]The corporate rule was published in the Federal Register as a final rulemaking on October 20, 2010, 75 Fed. Reg. 64786.

[2]See 75 Fed. Reg. 71526 (Nov. 24, 2010) (interim final rule with request for comments); 76 Fed. Reg. 16235 (Mar. 23, 2011) (final rule adopting the same technical corrections as the interim rule). NCUA proposed additional technical corrections and clarifications of the Corporate Rule in a proposed rulemaking published on September 6, 2011, 76 Fed. Reg. 54991.

Table 4: NCUA Corporate Rule through April 2011 Rulemaking

Issue	Corporate rule	Implementation status
Capital standards and prompt corrective action		
Capital standards[a]	A new set of capital standards for corporates was established, based generally on the Basel I capital requirements.[b] The new standards are: • Leverage ratio and tier-one RBC ratio: 4% or greater; and • Total RBC ratio: 8% or greater. The new standards replace the existing 4 percent mandatory minimum capital requirement.	The final rule was published on October 20, 2010. The new capital standards initially take partial effect one year after publication of the Rule (i.e., October 20, 2011) and are then phased in over 10 years[c]
Prompt corrective action	The rulemaking establishes a prompt corrective action (PCA) regime for corporates.[d] The corporate PCA system assigns corporates to one of five capital categories ranging from "well capitalized" to "critically undercapitalized." A corporate becomes subject to more severe supervisory actions and restrictions on its activities the lower it falls on the scale of capital categories. Prior to this, corporates were exempt from PCA.	The final rule was published on October 20, 2010, and effective as of October 20, 2011.
Investments, credit risk, and asset-liability management[e]		
Credit management[f]	Corporates are required to review all national recognized statistical rating organization (NRSRO) ratings.	The final rule was published on October 20, 2010, and effective as of January 18, 2011.
	Corporates are prohibited from investing in collateralized debt obligations, net interest margin securities, private-label MBS, or a security subordinated to any other securities in the issuance. A corporate holding investments that violate the new prohibitions once they took effect must submit an investment action plan to NCUA under 12 C.F.R. §704.10.	The final rule was published on October 20, 2010, and effective as of January 18, 2011.
	Corporate single obligor limits have been tightened to 25 percent of capital, except for several exemptions.	The final rule was published on October 20, 2010, and effective as of January 18, 2011.
Asset and liability management[g]	Imposes sector concentration limits on corporate investments.	The final rule was published on October 20, 2010, and effective as of January 18, 2011.
Corporate governance[h]		
Board representation[i]	All corporate board members are required to hold a chief executive officer, chief financial officer, or chief operating officer or treasurer/manager position at their member credit union or another member entity.	The final rule was published on October 20, 2010, and effective as of February 18, 2011.
	Individuals are prohibited from serving on the board of more than one corporate.	The final rule was published on October 20, 2010, and effective as of January 18, 2011.
	A majority of a corporate board's members are required to be representatives of credit unions.	The final rule was published on October 20, 2010, and will be effective as of October 21, 2013.

Issue	Corporate rule	Implementation status
Board and executive compensation[j]	Annual disclosure of amounts paid by corporates to its most highly compensated employees.	The final rule was published on October 20, 2010, and effective as of January 18, 2011.
	"Golden parachutes," are prohibited as defined as payments made to an "institution affiliated party" that are contingent on termination of that person's employment and received when the corporate making payment is troubled, undercapitalized, or insolvent.[k]	The final rule was published on October 20, 2010, and effective as of January 18, 2011.
	Corporates are prohibited from paying or reimbursing an institution affiliated party's legal or related expenses incurred in proceedings instituted by NCUA or a state regulator when that party is ultimately found liable.	The final rule was published on October 20, 2010, and effective as of January 18, 2011.
	Certain highly paid corporate executives are required to disclose compensation they receive from a corporate CUSO.[l]	The final rule was published as of April 29, 2011, and effective as of May 31, 2011.
Corporate board votes	The names of board members attending meetings are required to be recorded in the minutes along with the names of board members who voted "no" or abstained on any votes that were taken.[m]	The final rule was published on April 29, 2011, and effective as of May 31, 2011.
Corporate credit union service organizations (CUSOs)		
CUSO issues	Corporate CUSO activities are restricted to activities preapproved by NCUA.[n] The new rule grants approval for brokerage services and investment advisory services, and provides that NCUA may approve additional categories of activities and publish such approval on the agency website. Once granted, approval for an activity can only be withdrawn through a rulemaking.	The final rule was published on October 20, 2010, and effective as of January 18, 2011. However, CUSOs were given until April 18, 2011, to come into compliance with the activity restrictions.
	Corporates are required to divest from a CUSO that engages in unapproved activities.	The final rule was published and effective as of October 20, 2010, but, subject to certain conditions, corporate credit unions have until October 20, 2011, to divest from a noncomplying CUSO.[o]
	The new rule also requires CUSOs to permit their corporates as well as NCUA access to their books, records, personnel, equipment, and facilities.	The final rule was published on April 29, 2011, and effective as of May 31, 2011.
Corporate operations		
Liquidity[p]	Corporates are restricted from borrowing the lower of 10 times its capital or 50 percent of its capital and shares (excluding shares representing member reverse repurchase agreements).	The final rule was published on October 20, 2010, and effective as of January 18, 2011.[q]
	Corporate's secured borrowing is restricted to 30 days and for liquidity purposes. Securitized borrowing for nonliquidity purposes is limited to well-capitalized corporates and cannot exceed an amount equal to the corporate's excess capital.	The final rule was published on October 20, 2010, and effective as of January 18, 2011.

Issue	Corporate rule	Implementation status
Auditing and reporting requirements	Corporates are required to implement certain audit, reporting, and audit committee practices derived from the Federal Deposit Insurance Act, the Sarbanes-Oxley Act, and Federal Deposit Insurance Corporation regulations.[r]	The final rule was published on April 29, 2011, and effective dates as of January 1, 2012, for some of these requirements but others are delayed until 2013 and 2014.[s]
Enterprise risk management	Corporates are required to establish risk management policies and enterprise-wide risk management committees that included at least one independent risk management expert.[t]	The final rule was published on April 29, 2011, and effective April 29, 2013.
Fees	This rule authorizes corporates to charge their members reasonable one-time or periodic membership fees.[u]	The rule was published on April 29, 2011, and effective May 31, 2011.

Source: GAO summary of NCUA's corporate rule.

[a] 12 C.F.R. §704.3.

[b] Basel I is a set of international banking regulations put forth by the Basel Committee on Bank Supervision, which set out the minimum capital requirements of financial institutions with the goal of minimizing credit risk. Basel 1 requires banks to maintain a minimum amount (8 percent) of capital based on a percent of risk-weighted assets.

[c] See the preamble to the final rule, at 75 Fed. Reg. 64789-64792 and 64794-64802, for background on the new capital standards.

[d] 12 C.F.R. §704.4. The Corporate Rule also establishes procedures to govern corporate PCA-related determinations, codified at 12 C.F.R. §747.3001 through 3006. See the preamble at 75 Fed. Reg. 64792 and 64802-804 for background on the PCA provisions. In addition, the PCA system for corporates is similar in many (but not all) respects to the PCA system applicable to federally regulated and insured banking institutions as well as the PCA system applicable to natural person credit unions under section 207 of the Credit Union Act, 12 U.S.C. §1790d.

[e] 75 Fed. Reg. 64792

[f] 12 C.F.R. §704.6.

[g] 12 C.F.R. §704.8.

[h] For background, see 75 Fed. Reg. at 64793-94, 64811-17.

[i] 12 C.F.R. §704.14.

[j] Amends 12 C.F.R. §704.19.

[k] Amends 12 C.F.R. §704.20.

[l] The preamble to the final rule, 76 Fed. Reg. at 23862, gives background on this provision. This rule amends 12 C.F.R. §§704.11 and 704.19.

[m] See 76 Fed. Reg. at 23862-63 for background. Amended 12 C.F.R. §704.13.

[n] Amends 12 C.F.R. §704.11.

[o] For background on the CUSO provisions, see 75 Fed. Reg. 64794, 647811-13.

[p] Amended 12 C.F.R. §704.9.

[q] For background, see 75 Fed. Reg. at 64793, 647810-11.

[r] Amended 12 C.F.R. §704.15.

[s] For background, see 76 Fed. Reg. at 23863-64.

[t] Added a new section to the Corporate Rule, 12 C.F.R. §704.21.

[u] For background, see 76 Fed. Reg. at 23865-66. The rulemaking added a new section, 12 C.F.R. §704.22.

Appendix V: Comments from the National Credit Union Administration

 National Credit Union Administration

Office of the Chairman

December 19, 2011

Ms. A. Nicole Clowers
Director Financial Markets and Community Investment
United States Government Accountability Office
Washington, DC 20548

Dear Ms. Clowers:

The National Credit Union Administration (NCUA) reviewed the Government Accountability Office (GAO) draft report titled *National Credit Union Administration: Earlier Actions Are Needed to Better Address Troubled Credit Unions* (report) *(GAO-12-247)*. The report contains two recommendations. First, the report recommends the NCUA Chairman provide its Office of Inspector General (OIG) the necessary documentation to enable the OIG to verify the loss estimates for the Temporary Corporate Credit Union Stabilization Fund (Stabilization Fund). Second, the report recommends the NCUA Chairman consider additional triggers that would require early and forceful regulatory actions to improve the effectiveness of the Prompt Corrective Action (PCA) framework for credit unions, and make any corresponding recommendations to Congress.

NCUA agrees with both of the report's recommendations. In fact, I am pleased to report that year-end December 31, 2010, Stabilization Fund loss estimate documentation was finalized and provided to the OIG, as well as NCUA's external auditor, prior to December 1, 2011. NCUA will also be providing the finalized documentation for the June 30, 2011, loss estimates to the OIG before January 1, 2012.

Stabilization Fund Loss Estimates
As you know, the GAO audit work necessary to meet the statutory deadline for issuance of the report occurred while NCUA was still in the process of implementing some of the final stages of the Corporate System Resolution program. Thus, while much of the documentation was in final form, other components were only available in draft form as it was undergoing the necessary due diligence to be finalized. Regrettably, finalization of this documentation was a lengthy process and thus the December 31, 2010, audit for the Stabilization Fund has not yet been published. NCUA fully expects the publication of the audited financial statements in the very near future. Nevertheless, I believe it is important to put into context the additional time it took to complete this process.

1775 Duke Street - Alexandria, VA 22314-3428 - 703-518-6300 — 703-518-6319-Fax

Ms. A. Nicole Clowers
December 19, 2011
Page 2

The failures of several of the largest corporate credit unions created extraordinarily large and complex resolution issues. In addition, the resolution process occurred during a time when all financial institutions were under significant stress, creating supervisory and operational challenges for NCUA on many fronts. The failed corporate credit unions had assets totaling

$106 billion[1] and were the backbone of operations for most natural person credit unions. In addition to the assertive steps taken by NCUA to stabilize the corporate credit union system and ensure the continued operation of consumer credit unions, the agency immediately began work to devise a solution to isolate and fund the distressed assets. As the report notes, starting in the fourth quarter of 2010 NCUA took comprehensive actions of a large scale and high degree of complexity, including the NCUA Guaranteed Notes (NGN) securitization program, to achieve an orderly, least cost resolution for these institutions. NCUA has been successful in this massive undertaking and accomplished this feat in a responsible way.

Under the Corporate System Resolution program, NCUA re-securitized almost $50 billion in distressed investment securities held by the failed corporate credit unions. These distressed securities, sometimes referred to by NCUA as legacy assets, included over 2,600 complex securities. As part of the NGN program, NCUA executed 13 securitization transactions to fund these legacy assets in the market. The complex and time consuming process of issuing the NGNs was ongoing from October of 2010 through June of 2011, during the year-end audit period.

In the summer of 2010 Barclays Capital was hired as lead advisor and bookrunner to facilitate the disposition of the legacy assets. As part of the securitization process Barclays Capital aided in providing market values and intrinsic values for the legacy assets as of the securitization date.[2] However, the contract with Barclays did not include providing valuations necessary for the preparation of year-end financial statements.

NCUA needed a platform to support ongoing financial reporting for the Stabilization Fund for the duration of the NGNs (2021), including assessment of subsequent events in 2011 for the 2010 Stabilization Fund financial statements. Thus, on January 7, 2011, NCUA published a solicitation for a vendor to aid in ongoing valuation of and reporting on the legacy assets. Blackrock Solutions, a leading firm in the field, was awarded the contract on April 27, 2011. As a result, the extensive analytical and due diligence process for determining December 31, 2010, values for the legacy assets did not begin until well into 2011.

To ensure accurate financial reporting, NCUA invested in new tools, hired experts, and engaged leading industry specialists including accounting and valuation experts as the report notes. These experts aided in determining the values and expected losses from the failed corporate credit unions, including assets re-securitized into the NGNs.[3] These necessary and purposeful actions

---

[1] As of January 1, 2008.
[2] Barclays Capital modeled the securities to project principal and interest cash flows over the life of the legacy assets, which included estimated expected losses (principal defaults).
[3] As the report notes, at its August 2011 meeting the NCUA Board also established formal oversight for the NGN program and related underlying legacy assets through creation of the NGN Securities Management and Oversight Committee.

Ms. A. Nicole Clowers
December 19, 2011
Page 3

slowed the audit work, as NCUA emphasized accuracy and reliability over speed while standing up this new and complex process in 2011. This included incorporation of necessary internal controls to ensure that the final published financial statements accurately reflect corporate stabilization costs.

While the Stabilization Fund audit was not final in time to meet the GAO audit work timeline, the results from the valuation experts were completed and available. The valuation results are the primary basis for the vast majority of the loss projections. Based on these results, as of June 30, 2011, NCUA projects total future Stabilization Fund assessments to credit unions in the range of $1.9 billion to $6.2 billion over the remaining life of the Stabilization Fund (2012 to 2021). With over $95 billion in net worth in the credit union system and annual pre-assessment net income of over $8 billion,[4] the credit union system has ample capacity to pay these costs over the remaining life of the Stabilization Fund.[5] Therefore, it is highly improbable the taxpayer would be subject to any loss.[6]

In summary, during 2011 NCUA has consulted closely with various experts and our external auditors to apply generally accepted accounting principles to complex securities transactions. With systems, processes, and personnel now in place, the agency is committed to having future audits completed in a shorter timeframe and providing additional levels of transparency for the loss estimates and performance of the legacy assets.[7]

Prompt Corrective Action Effectiveness
The report's second recommendation is for the NCUA Chairman to consider additional triggers that would require early and forceful regulatory actions to improve the effectiveness of the Prompt Corrective Action (PCA) framework for credit unions, and make any corresponding recommendations to Congress. NCUA agrees with this recommendation and is committed to continued research and analysis in this area. In fact, as part of the comprehensive modernization of NCUA's regulations I initiated, NCUA has plans for next year to study potential enhancements to PCA regulations related to risk-based net worth standards for consumer credit unions.

---

[4] Based on annualized September 30, 2011, pre-assessment net income.
[5] NCUA designed and built a 10 year loss impact model specifically to analyze the impact of Stabilization Fund costs on credit union capital, earnings, and liquidity under base and stress scenarios. This model has been in place since the third quarter of 2010 and is updated regularly.
[6] The following information is as of June 30, 2011. The unpaid principal balance of the legacy assets underlying the NGNs is $37.4 billion and their market value is $22 billion. Blackrock's calculation of the net realizable value for these assets is $27.6 billion. The outstanding NGN investor balance to be serviced by cash flows from the underlying legacy asset is $26.5 billion. Thus, the potential need for guarantee payments to be made by NCUA on the NGNs is finite and manageable relative to the credit union systems' ability to absorb any needed increase in Stabilization Fund assessments.
[7] NCUA has been working for several months on a website designed to provide greater details for Stabilization Fund stakeholders on the legacy assets and loss estimates. This website is expected to be completed soon.

Ms. A. Nicole Clowers
December 19, 2011
Page 4

NCUA will also consider the extent to which additional triggers could be identified for the net
worth requirement (i.e., leverage ratio). As the recommendation recognizes, however, the PCA
provisions for the net worth requirement for consumer credit unions is largely explicitly
established by statute. Therefore any potential enhancements in this specific area will require
Congressional action.

While acknowledging the limitations of capital as the primary measure in the PCA framework, it
is also important to underscore the care that needs to be taken in identifying alternatives and
extensions to the framework. A number of examples cited in the report have potential
drawbacks, not the least of which is that the vast majority of credit unions meeting the cited
conditions are not under distress or likely to fail. In developing potential enhancements NCUA
will be guided by the following principles: (1) PCA triggers and corrective actions should be
predictable and based on broadly applicable metrics; and (2) PCA triggers and corrective actions
should reduce the likelihood and cost of failure.

As you may be aware, I currently chair the Federal Financial Institutions Examination Council
and serve on the Financial Stability Oversight Council with the federal banking agencies. As
such, NCUA is following the related developments of the federal banking agencies'
consideration of enhancements to PCA triggers as recommended in GAO's report *Banking
Regulation: Modified Prompt Corrective Action Framework Would Improve Effectiveness*
(GAO-11-612).

Regarding NCUA intervention when a credit union's financial condition is deteriorating, it is
important to address a potential misconception in the report. NCUA has recognized the need for
timelier use of formal enforcement action as noted in the agency's responses to the OIG material
loss reviews (MLRs) cited in the report. However, nearly all failed credit unions received an
enforceable regulatory action prior to failure, either through PCA or non-PCA authorities, with
certain cases occurring so abruptly that longer lead time for action prior to failure was not
possible.[8] NCUA has a strong record of employing PCA actions when credit unions trip the
related PCA triggers, as PCA actions are often more expedient forms of enforceable regulatory
action.

It is also worthy to note that consumer credit unions performed very well during the worst
financial crisis since the Great Depression, and NCUA was highly successful overall in
mitigating failures and losses for consumer credit unions. The 85 consumer credit union failures
occurred over a two and a half year period during the height of the economic crisis. As noted in
the report, the level of annualized failures is relatively low, only marginally higher than pre-crisis
levels, and involved institutions with less than 1% of total credit union assets. NCUA was
effective in prioritizing our supervisory resources during the economic crisis to prevent the
failure of larger credit unions that came under stress, and in mitigating losses for those that did

---

[8] Of the 11 failures out of the 85 for which there was no enforcement action prior to failure, 5 were fraud
cases which required immediate action and 6 were cases where the credit union's financial health
deteriorated very abruptly.

Ms. A. Nicole Clowers
December 19, 2011
Page 5

fail. The National Credit Union Share Insurance Fund insuring consumer credit unions remains healthy and strong, with an equity ratio of over 1.32% as of November 30, 2011.

NCUA appreciates the professionalism of the GAO review team that prepared the report. Thank you for the opportunity to comment.

Sincerely,

Debbie Matz
Chairman

Appendix VI: GAO Contact and Staff Acknowledgments

GAO Contact	A. Nicole Clowers, (202) 512-8678 or clowersa@gao.gov
Staff Acknowledgments	In addition to the contacts named above, Debra R. Johnson, Assistant Director; Emily R. Chalmers; Gary P. Chupka; Nima Patel Edwards; Debra Hoffman; Barry A. Kirby; Colleen A. Moffatt; Timothy C. Mooney; Robert A. Rieke; and Gregory J. Ziombra made significant contributions to this report. Other contributors included Pamela R. Davidson, Michael E. Hoffman, Grant M. Mallie, Jessica M. Sandler, and Henry Wray.

GAO's Mission	The Government Accountability Office, the audit, evaluation, and investigative arm of Congress, exists to support Congress in meeting its constitutional responsibilities and to help improve the performance and accountability of the federal government for the American people. GAO examines the use of public funds; evaluates federal programs and policies; and provides analyses, recommendations, and other assistance to help Congress make informed oversight, policy, and funding decisions. GAO's commitment to good government is reflected in its core values of accountability, integrity, and reliability.
Obtaining Copies of GAO Reports and Testimony	The fastest and easiest way to obtain copies of GAO documents at no cost is through GAO's website (www.gao.gov). Each weekday afternoon, GAO posts on its website newly released reports, testimony, and correspondence. To have GAO e-mail you a list of newly posted products, go to www.gao.gov and select "E-mail Updates."
Order by Phone	The price of each GAO publication reflects GAO's actual cost of production and distribution and depends on the number of pages in the publication and whether the publication is printed in color or black and white. Pricing and ordering information is posted on GAO's website, http://www.gao.gov/ordering.htm.
	Place orders by calling (202) 512-6000, toll free (866) 801-7077, or TDD (202) 512-2537.
	Orders may be paid for using American Express, Discover Card, MasterCard, Visa, check, or money order. Call for additional information.
Connect with GAO	Connect with GAO on Facebook, Flickr, Twitter, and YouTube. Subscribe to our RSS Feeds or E-mail Updates. Listen to our Podcasts. Visit GAO on the web at www.gao.gov.
To Report Fraud, Waste, and Abuse in Federal Programs	Contact: Website: www.gao.gov/fraudnet/fraudnet.htm E-mail: fraudnet@gao.gov Automated answering system: (800) 424-5454 or (202) 512-7470
Congressional Relations	Katherine Siggerud, Managing Director, SiggerudK@gao.gov, (202) 512-4400, U.S. Government Accountability Office, 441 G Street NW, Room 7125, Washington, DC 20548
Public Affairs	Chuck Young, Managing Director, youngc1@gao.gov, (202) 512-4800 U.S. Government Accountability Office, 441 G Street NW, Room 7149 Washington, DC 20548

Please Print on Recycled Paper.